D1224579

# OCEB Certification Guide

# OCEB Certification Guide

## Business Process Management – Fundamental Level

**Tim Weilkiens**
**Christian Weiss**
**Andrea Grass**

AMSTERDAM • BOSTON • HEIDELBERG • LONDON
NEW YORK • OXFORD • PARIS • SAN DIEGO
SAN FRANCISCO • SINGAPORE • SYDNEY • TOKYO
Morgan Kaufmann is an imprint of Elsevier

ELSEVIER

Acquiring Editor: Rachel Roumeliotis
Development Editor: Robyn Day
Project Manager: Jessica Vaughan
Designer: Joanne Blank

*Morgan Kaufmann* is an imprint of Elsevier
225 Wyman Street, Waltham, MA 02451, USA

© 2011 Elsevier, Inc. All rights reserved.

No part of this publication may be reproduced or transmitted in any form or by any means, electronic or mechanical, including photocopying, recording, or any information storage and retrieval system, without permission in writing from the publisher. Details on how to seek permission, further information about the Publisher's permissions policies and our arrangements with organizations such as the Copyright Clearance Center and the Copyright Licensing Agency, can be found at our website: www.elsevier.com/permissions.

This book and the individual contributions contained in it are protected under copyright by the Publisher (other than as may be noted herein).

Notices
Knowledge and best practice in this field are constantly changing. As new research and experience broaden our understanding, changes in research methods or professional practices, may become necessary. Practitioners and researchers must always rely on their own experience and knowledge in evaluating and using any information or methods described herein. In using such information or methods they should be mindful of their own safety and the safety of others, including parties for whom they have a professional responsibility.

To the fullest extent of the law, neither the Publisher nor the authors, contributors, or editors, assume any liability for any injury and/or damage to persons or property as a matter of products liability, negligence or otherwise, or from any use or operation of any methods, products, instructions, or ideas contained in the material herein.

Library of Congress Cataloging-in-Publication Data
Weilkiens, Tim.
  [Basiswissen Geschäftsprozessmanagement. English]
  OCEB certification guide : business process management, fundamental level / Tim Weilkiens, Christian Weiss, Andrea Grass.
    p. cm.
  ISBN 978-0-12-386985-2
  1. Business consultants–Certification. 2. Electronic data processing personnel–Certification. 3. Industrial management–Examinations–Study guides. 4. Management information systems–Examinations–Study guides. I. Weiss, Christian. II. Grass, Andrea R. III. Title.
  HD69.C6W445 2010
  658.50076–dc23

                                    2011018468

British Library Cataloguing-in-Publication Data
A catalogue record for this book is available from the British Library.

ISBN: 978-0-12-386985-2

Printed in the United States of America
11  12  13  14  15     10  9  8  7  6  5  4  3  2  1

**Working together to grow
libraries in developing countries**

www.elsevier.com | www.bookaid.org | www.sabre.org

ELSEVIER    BOOK AID
            International    Sabre Foundation

For information on all MK publications visit our website at www.mkp.com

# Contents

**Tim Weilkiens** is area manager of Systems Engineering of the German consulting company, oose Innovative Informatik GmbH. His work focuses on modeling and development processes. He represents oose GmbH at OMG, where he, among other things, actively contributes to the UML specification. He is the co-author of the SysML specification and developer of the OCEB certification program.

**Christian Weiss** is CEO of oose Innovative Informatik GmbH. Since 1991, he has worked in object-oriented software development as executive developer, consultant, and trainer. He regularly gives lectures at conferences and universities. His work focuses on business process modeling and agile project management. In particular, he supports large enterprises in the process analysis and design and implementation of corresponding methodologies.

**Andrea Grass** works as a consultant and trainer at oose Innovative Informatik GmbH. Her work focuses on business process modeling and object-oriented software development. This particularly includes the design and implementation of new or adapted methodologies in enterprises.

# Preface

Little did I know or even suspect, when I started organizing OMG's project to certify practitioners of BPMN modeling, how ambitious a project we would end up with. But as OMG's group of BPM experts and I started to define a set of certifications and levels, the scope of the project expanded, seemingly of its own accord, on two fronts: First, it grew to embrace a host of roles involved in running the business side of an enterprise, including interacting in real time with other enterprises, and second, as our group of BPM experts delighted in reminding me, the field of BPM itself divides into two groups, Business and Technical, each with its own set of objectives and skills, needing its own set of certifications. We ended up calling the program OCEB–OMG Certified Expert in BPM. But does BPM in this case refer to Business Process Management or Business Process Modeling? Well, in this case, it refers to both, since the program covers both and, with five examinations and levels, has enough space to do the job properly.

To see what I'm talking about, think about the OCEB examination structure. Most noticeable is the division into Business and Technical tracks for the upper two levels, but we're going to focus on the Fundamental level at the bottom. It's the subject of this book, of course, but let's consider its importance as a foundation for the upper levels of the program.

You can see the seven major examination topics in the Contents of this book, or on the OCEB web site. They fall into three major categories:

- The business itself
- Business Process Modeling using BPMN
- Frameworks for process quality, business governance, and metrics

OMG's team of BPM experts included business-oriented topics at this level to ensure that everyone (since this certification is a prerequisite for every other OCEB level) who displays an OCEB certification logo is familiar with the basic concepts of business goals and objectives, ways and means, and so on that will be represented in business process diagrams and bring in the money to pay everyone's salary. These topics are already familiar to most of the folks who work on the business side, but will be new to many of the technical people.

Business Process Modeling using BPMN is well covered—OMG's team of question-writing experts included many of the principal authors of the BPMN specification itself. Divided into two major topics, BP Modeling Concepts and BP Modeling Skills, this part of the certification tests both knowledge of BPMN language elements and, using brief scenarios, familiarity with model building and model reading. This level includes only basic parts of BPMN—we've left plenty for the more advanced levels to cover!

The final section, on Frameworks for Process Quality, Business Governance, and Metrics, surveys a range of frameworks with which BPM practitioners need to be familiar. OCEB Certified individuals should be aware of all of these frameworks, since one or another may be helpful or even necessary in BPM work, depending on one's area of practice. However, this examination does not test the ability to work with any of them—after all, each is (or could be) the subject of its own dedicated certification! At this level, we thought that an awareness of the names, scopes, and goals of a wide range of frameworks would provide our certified candidates with the knowledge they need in their practices.

This coverage, and the examination questions themselves, were all written by a team of more than 25 BPM experts listed on the OCEB Authors Page at http://www.omg.org/oceb/authors.htm. On this page you'll find the name of Tim Weilkiens, the author of this book. Tim was an active contributor throughout the project, earning the right to display the OCEB Content Developer logo on this book. As project leader, I appreciated Tim's timely and high-quality contributions. As a candidate for the OCEB Fundamental certification, you'll appreciate his familiarity with the coverage and material, and his ability to collect and digest the many references into a single volume.

As you study your way through this book, and through a course if you've decided to take one, concentrate on developing your BPMN (and BMM!) modeling skills and absorbing the material so you can build your BPM career. Of course you're concerned with what will be on the test, but the question that our team of experts asked before we put anything on the test was "Is this important to the work of a BPM practitioner?" so you can be sure that all of your study will enhance your career as it prepares you for the OCEB Fundamental examination.

Let me personally wish you the best as you prepare to take the OCEB Fundamental examination. I know you'll be proud to display the OCEB Certified logo on your business card and resume, and hope that you'll come back to our program and certify at one or both higher levels in your career track, or perhaps even both tracks if your role is BPM Guru.

Jon Siegel, PhD
Vice President, Technology Transfer, and Director, Certification OMG
December 2009

# CHAPTER 1
# Getting Started

This is not the end. It is not even the beginning of the end. But it is, perhaps, the end of the beginning.

**Winston Churchill**

## SENSE AND NONSENSE OF CERTIFICATIONS

Since you are holding this book in your hands, presumably you think that certifications make sense—at least the certification OMG Certified Expert in Business Process Management (OCEB) of the Object Management Group (OMG). The subject of certification is discussed rather controversially and emotionally. The goal of this section is to take an objective look at the pros and cons of certifications. The subsequent sections are then dedicated to the OCEB certification and its contents.

The arguments in favor and against certifications are representative for certificates with automated tests without any initial requirements. Certificates that not only examine knowledge but also test skills—for instance, in the course of an oral examination or by demanding initial requirements, like a proof of practical experience—may have different arguments.

These certificates basically involve a measurable proof of knowledge. Let's assume you want to hire consultants in the area of Business Process Management (BPM). How do you determine in advance which BPM knowledge the people have? Professional qualifications rather prove holistic skills than topic-specific knowledge such as BPM. An OCEB certificate is a tiny little piece to solve this issue. Of course, you must not consider the certificate separately, and even less does it replace a one-to-one interview.

Knowledge is subject to half life—you forget things that you don't use regularly. For this reason, there are certificates that have an expiration date. After this expiration date, you must repeat the examination and pay for it to renew the certificate. This is very profitable for those issuing the certificates, and everyone may have his or her own opinion as to what extent these repeated examinations make sense (for instance, for pilot licenses), or whether the date of the first examination and some knowledge on the projects implemented are sufficient to get a good idea of how up-to-date the knowledge actually is. In any case, the OCEB certificates are valid indefinitely.

In real life, certificates are frequently misinterpreted and occasionally misused. Someone who doesn't know anything about the content or implementation of a certificate may easily be misled by alleged knowledge, skills, and experience, which most certificates don't prove at all. For example, an analyst requires the ability to abstract, analytic power, excellent communication skills, and other soft skills.

These skills are not covered by the OCEB certificates, and they could not be checked by any other multiple choice test. This way, skills can only be verified to a limited extent or not at all. A certificate like OCEB is only a measure for knowledge—no more, no less.

It can be clearly perceived that the demand for certificates has increased in recent years. Certificates exist because there's a requirement for them. They don't grow on trees. One of the requirements has been shown previously—the requirement to make knowledge measurable. But there are further interests and the associated stakeholders.

The person certified possibly doesn't want to be measured at all. Maybe he wants to use the certificate to increase his value in order to increase his prospects for a good job or a profitable assignment. Or he perceives the certificate as a privilege. E-mail signatures frequently provide a proud list of all certificates achieved.

Supervisors are also stakeholders in the certification business. Maybe they want to use the certifications to upgrade their teams to the outside to be more successful in customer acquisition. As trainers for various certifications, we often see that supervisors want to use certifications to test their employees or make target agreements that are relevant for their salary. When the participants introduce themselves during our preparatory course they often say, "My boss wants me to do this." Alternatively, there are also managers who don't pay for their employees' certification because they dread fluctuation or higher salary demands due to the gain in status of the employee.

The list of stakeholders wouldn't be complete without the certification organization itself. For OCEB, these include OMG and UML[1] Technology Institute Co., Ltd (UTI), which developed the certification program and assume responsibility for it. There is no financial interest here. The revenues are to cover the costs for developing the certificate. However, OMG provides certificates to enable its members to earn money, for instance, with preparatory courses and consulting services in the topic area of the respective certificate. Persons running test centers also earn money. All examinations of OMG and thus OCEB are done in Pearson VUE test centers.

---

[1]United Modeling Language

A certificate is only one tiny little portion of many factors to assess a person. Depending on the context, it can be an important or unimportant little piece or simply the final touch to round off a person's image.

## THE OCEB CERTIFICATION PROGRAM

The certification program, OMG Certified Expert in Business Process Management (OCEB), offers five certificates that prove expertise in the BPM area. It is the third certification program of OMG after the OMG Certified UML Professional (OCUP) and OMG Certified Real-time and Embedded Specialist (OCRES) certification programs. The standardization consortium is primarily associated with UML, Model Driven Architectures (MDA), and Common Object Request Broker Architecture (CORBA). That's where you can find the roots of OMG. In the meantime, however, a considerable tree of standards has grown out of other areas. Besides systems engineering with OMG Systems Modeling Language (SysML), the consortium has also moved into the discipline of business process management. OMG is responsible for many significant standards from this area including Business Process Modeling Notation (BPMN), Business Process Maturity Model (BPMM), and Business Motivation Model (BMM).

These and other BPM standards provide support to discover, incorporate, optimize, and implement business processes. The goal of OCEB is to provide a measure of this knowledge [17]. The certification program has been developed by a team of international experts. These include, for example, the OMG's project leader, Jon Siegel, Stephen White from IBM, as well as Markus Klink and Tim Weilkiens from oose Innovative Informatik GmbH. You can find a full list of participants on OCEB's official web site, http://www.omg.org/oceb [18].

OCEB not only addresses standards of OMG, but also asks questions on general knowledge of project and business process management, business administration, business rules, and quality frameworks like Basel II or Six Sigma.

Accordingly, the reference list not only comprises OMG specifications, but also various articles and books. The list is rather comprehensive because, so far, no individual book has been published that covers such a wide range of topics in the area of business processes. But don't worry, only individual sections from these books are referenced and not all hundreds of pages. Moreover, you are holding a preparatory book in your hands that fully covers the topics relevant for OCEB Fundamental. You only require the official references if you want to read the original or require additional information.

There are five OCEB certificates in total (Table 1.1). The Fundamental level covers basic knowledge. This forms the basis from which OCEB branches into technical and business tracks. The technical certificates are intended for IT employees who implement business processes in systems; that is, architects, designers, and developers. Topics include, for example, detailed modeling aspects, information security, and architectures such as Service Oriented Architecture (SOA). The business certificates address analysts, architects, and also

| Table 1.1 | OCEB Certification Program | |
|---|---|---|
| **OCEB Profile** | | |
| Name | OMG Certified Expert in Business Process Management | |
| Target Group | Business analysts and architects, software designers and developers | |
| Levels | \ Fundamental | |
| | ʌBusiness Intermediate | Technical Intermediate |
| | ʌBusiness Advanced | Technical Advanced |
| Prerequisites | None | |
| Test Environment | Pearson VUE test center | |
| | Multiple choice | |
| Language | English | |
| Validity | Unlimited | |
| | Identical on an international scale | |

employees of specialist departments. Topics comprise, for example, change management, process improvement, and the management of business processes.

The following sections briefly present the individual levels. Starting with Chapter 2, we deal only with the topics of the Fundamental level.

 ## OCEB Fundamental

The lowest level of the certification program bridges the gap between the IT department and the analyst teams or specialist departments. It creates a uniform understanding for terms, concepts, methods, and modeling of business processes. The following topic areas are covered. The percentages each indicate the weighting in the certification process.

- Business goals, objectives (8%)
- Business process concepts and fundamentals (11%)
- Business process management concepts and fundamentals (10%)
- Business modeling (16%)
- Business process modeling concepts (16%)
- Business process modeling skills (24%)
- Process quality, governance, and metrics frameworks (15%)

The enterprise goals topic area covers concepts of business administration, marketing, and project management. Anyone who works in the business process environment should have basic knowledge of organizational forms of enterprises, market environment analyses, marketing, financial key figures, and business analysis methods.

Independent of standards like BPMN, the topic areas concepts and fundamentals of business processes or business process management require basic knowledge of business processes. Not only the What, but also the How is important; for example, how to discover business processes or present business process hierarchies, and how to handle the various degrees of abstraction in the description. By aligning the business processes with the enterprise goals, a link is established between the first and the third topic areas.

The business modeling topic area is the first to address the OMG specifications. The BMM is a standard to describe business plans. It defines the basic business concepts, their characteristics, and their interrelations. This includes vision, mission, strategy, business rules, objectives, influencers, and appraisals.

The business process management concepts and fundamentals topic area deals with the handling of business processes in enterprises, the impacts of process-focused structures, and the various approaches of business process management such as Business Process Reengineering (BPR) or Total Quality Management (TQM). Another topic covered here is the OMG standard, BPMM. This is a maturity model for business processes, similar to Capability Maturity Model Integration (CMMI) for software and system development.

With 40 percent, the business process modeling concepts and skills topics assume the largest part of the OCEB Fundamental certification. The OMG standard, BPMN, predominates here. BPMN fundamentals and the diagram elements of Business Process Diagram (BPD) are required here. You not only need to know what a specific element represents, but also must be able to interpret a BPD. You must be able to answer questions on BPD with real subject-matter knowledge.

The last topic area of the OCEB Fundamental certification deals with process quality, governance, and metrics frameworks.

## OCEB Business Intermediate

The Business Intermediate level comprises six topic areas:

- Intermediate business motivational modeling (10%)
- Organization structure (5%)
- Business process modeling with BPMN (34%)
- Business process management knowledge and skills (20%)
- Process quality and governance frameworks (17%)
- Business rules approach (14%)

Topic areas from the Fundamental level are repeated here. They are further advanced. For example, the various topic areas are supplemented as follows: further concepts of BMM in business modeling; additional elements and concepts of BPMN in business process modeling, for instance, patterns, choreography, and orchestration; and IT Infrastructure Library (ITIL) or more detailed topics on Six Sigma for process quality and governance frameworks.

The organization structures topic is new. In addition to general questions, this also involves an emerging OMG standard, Organization Structure Metamodel (OSM). The business process management knowledge and skills topic deals with measuring and optimizing business processes using Key Performance

Indicators (KPI), Critical Success Factors (CSF), and Balanced Scorecards. It comprises the documentation and simulation of business processes, the monitoring of statuses and results of business processes (Business Activity Monitoring (BAM)), and the basics of a Business Process Management Center of Excellence (CoE). The business rules topic covers general approaches, but also concrete OMG standards such as Semantics Business Vocabulary and Rules (SBVR).

 ## OCEB Business Advanced

The Business Advanced level also comprises six topic areas:

- Aligning BPM with enterprise goals and resources (11%)
- Advanced business process modeling with BPMN (15%)
- Management of BPM programs (27%)
- Advanced change management (11%)
- Compliance and assurance (22%)
- Advanced topics in process improvement (14%)

BPM—generally a main area of the OCEB certification program—is covered in more detail. This involves the handling of large models, the validation of models, and the methodology of discovering processes.

The second topic area, aligning BPM with enterprise goals and resources, discusses SOA and Enterprise Decision Management (EDM) among other topics. Enterprise architectures, team organization, and business cases are topics for managing the BPM programs. Advanced change management deals with general principles of how to implement changes in organizations. The fifth topic area, compliance and assurance, covers Governance, Risk, and Compliance (GRC); Corporate Social Responsibility (CSR); and information security. Finally, the advanced topics of process improvement deal with Six Sigma and BPMM again.

 ## OCEB Technical Intermediate

The technical track addresses the technical world of business processes, for instance, application architectures such as SOA or workflow management systems. This also includes topics of the business track, but the focus is on technology now. OCEB thus bridges these two worlds by certifying a common understanding of the terminology used.

The Technical Intermediate level comprises seven topic areas:

- Business process management awareness (10%)
- Business process modeling with BPMN (31%)
- Workflow pattern (7%)
- Business rules (16%)
- Architecture topics (13%)
- IT infrastructure and business process (13%)
- Monitoring and managing processes (10%)

Business process management coverage in this technical track examination concentrates on BPM systems rather than management practices. However, this coverage does not extend to specific products.

One core area of this certification level is on business process modeling with BPMN, with 31 percent. This covers advanced constructs of BPMN. The architecture topics naturally deal not only with SOA, but also with Model Driven Architectures (MDA). ITIL, Service Level Agreements (SLA), and Control Objectives for Information and Related Technology (COBIT) are included in the IT infrastructures topic, and the handling of process data and BAM is part of the topic, monitoring and managing processes.

## OCEB Technical Advanced

The Technical Advanced level also covers seven topic areas:

- Business process management awareness (13%)
- Advanced business process modeling with BPMN (25%)
- Understanding metamodeling concepts (9%)
- Enterprise architecture (23%)
- Business rules (8%)
- Implementation and integration (9%)
- Vendor selection and marketplace topics (13%)

Topics covered in the Intermediate level are discussed in further detail in the Advanced level. For example, the business process management awareness topic deals with KPI and BMM; the advanced business process modeling with BPMN involves model optimization, Business Process Execution Language (BPEL), BAM, and Enterprise Services Bus (ESB). The business rules topic queries the Production Rules Representation (PRR) OMG standard and the Rete algorithm, among other things.

The metamodeling topic requires basic knowledge of the structure of modeling languages in general. The enterprise architecture topic area covers SOA and patterns as well as the ISO 38500 and IEEE 1028 standards. The implementation and integration topic area involves Enterprise Resource Planning (ERP), Customer Relationship Management (CRM), Software as a Service (SaaS), legacy systems, and Data Warehouse. The topic area of vendor selection and marketplace topics does not discuss concrete products, but the process of tool selection; for instance, cost-benefit analysis, Return on Investment (ROI), and requests for proposals.

## OBJECT MANAGEMENT GROUP

This section briefly introduces you to the organization that stands behind the OCEB certification program.

The OMG is an international standardization organization. Since 1989, it has developed and managed standards in various disciplines and domains such as software development, systems engineering, business process management, financials, authorities, healthcare, robotics, and many more. The best-known standards include CORBA, UML, OMG SysML, and BPMN.

Any organization can join OMG and actively participate in the standardization process. Almost all large enterprises of the IT industry and many small companies as well as universities are represented in OMG.

Each year, OMG organizes conferences and technical meetings, where the various task teams come together to discuss and adopt standards.

With the implementation of UML 2.0 in 2003, OMG for the first time developed a certification program called OCUP to provide a scale for the knowledge about one of its standards. This was followed by OCRES in 2006 for standards and general knowledge in the area of real-time and embedded systems. OCEB was developed and published as the third certification program in 2008. The certification program OCSMP on OMG SysML has just been published.

## CERTIFICATION PROCESS

The first step on the path to certification is the contentual preparation (Figure 1.1). The topics covered by the certification are specified by OMG in the coverage map (see the appendix). The spectrum of topics is very diversified. Accordingly, the list of books, articles, and specifications, which are part of the official reference list of OCEB Fundamental, is very long. It takes a lot of effort to read and understand all of these references. And it also involves some rather significant costs, which will make the bookseller of your choice very happy. We've prepared these topics in a compressed form and wrote this book on the basic knowledge for business process management.

Furthermore, we (the authors) have extensive experience with the OCEB certification. Tim even participated in the development of the tests. He was a member

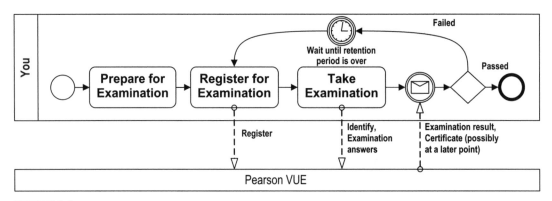

**FIGURE 1.1**
Certification Process

of the small committee that determined the topical coverage of the exams, and wrote many of the original questions. Oose Innovative Informatik GmbH was the first enterprise in Germany to offer preparatory courses. This way, we were able to get profound insight into the experiences of our participants.

We compiled the information in this book based on this experience. Note, however, that although we know the actual questions, we won't pass them on because then the test and the certificate would become worthless, aside from the fact that this would be illegal. It is therefore not sufficient to just read this book or learn everything by heart—this book is supposed to be a guide to gain BPM basic knowledge.

Taking the examination is the easiest step on the road to the OCEB certification. Go to the web site of OMG certification at Pearson VUE, http://www.pearsonvue.com/omg; search for a test center nearby; and register for an exam. Specific professional prerequisites, such as a university degree, are not necessary. The examination fee is about $200.

You must take a computer-based exam to obtain OCEB certificates. Participants must report to the test center and identify themselves 30 minutes before the test begins. Formally, two IDs (for example, ID card and driver's license) are required. One of these IDs must have a photograph. At the test center, the participants are briefly instructed on how to use the test software. Then the test starts, and the countdown begins.

The test includes multiple choice questions that must be answered within a predefined period of time. The questions come from a large pool and are always recombined so that the tests are all unique. The questions are subject to secrecy, and the test center doesn't know them either.

Each of the five OCEB certification exams includes 90 questions. You have 90 minutes to complete the exam. The questions are all in English. If English is not your native language, you are granted another 30 minutes (it is rightly assumed that you require more time to understand the English questions and answers).

Each question is provided on a separate screen, and you can scroll back and forth between the questions. Most will find it easier to answer the questions in the sequence in which they are presented, but you can also skip questions and answer them later. You have the option to set a little flag for questions that you want to review later. At the end of the exam, a review screen lets you see which questions still need to be answered and for which questions you've set a flag.

At the end of each chapter of this book are test questions that are similar to the original question of the certification. These enable you to get a feel for the types of questions, and you can check your current state of knowledge.

The test room is under video surveillance or monitored directly by test center staff. You cannot bring any aids; even paper or pens are not allowed. The test center provides a rigid memo board and erasable marker for temporary notes, which must be returned after completion. If participants violate these rules, they automatically fail. The staff running the test center are also subject to strict requirements and controls.

You will pass the Fundamental exam if you answer at least 55 out of 90 questions correctly (approximately 60%). The passing scores for other OCEB exams are similar, but not exactly the same. The result is available immediately, and if you passed, you receive a preliminary certificate to take along with you. The official document (in color for the picture frame behind your desk) is delivered by mail later.

If you've failed a test, you must wait at least 21 days to repeat the exam. A maximum of three attempts is permitted within 12 months.

The five certification levels are based on one another; that is, you only obtain a higher certificate if you've successfully passed the previous one. So it is not possible to pass only the OCEB Business Advanced test to receive the certificate.

Also plan to put your acquired knowledge into practice. In the short term, your only goal may be to pass the exam, but surely you also have medium-term goals with regard to your BPM knowledge and skills. You will invest a lot of energy to build up this knowledge. Utilize this basis to improve yourself in practice. The best way to preserve book learning is to use it in practice.

## Other Certification Programs

There are a myriad of certification programs, but only a few in the business process environment. OMG established the OCEB certification program for a reason. This program did not follow any trend, but filled a gap.

## Case Study

In this book, we often refer to the case study of the company SpeedyCar to explain the topics with a practical orientation. To understand the context, the following briefly introduces this example.

The car rental company SpeedyCar has set itself the goal to minimize employment of staff through innovative IT systems and thus be able to offer unbeatable prices in the market. Of course, the service must not fall by the wayside. Quite the contrary—the service is supposed to be considerably better and more visible for customers compared to competitors. One specific feature of SpeedyCar is that only registered customers can use the services.

In return, they receive particularly favorable prices toward conventional car rental companies.

SpeedyCar commissions oose Innovative Informatik GmbH to perform an actual and target analysis of their business and its processes. The results form the basis for the future strategic orientation of the company.

The actual and target analysis is not discussed continuously in this book, but we will focus on the contents of the OCEB Fundamental certification and show sections that depict the current topic.

Besides OCEB, Certified Business Analysis Professional (CBAP) of International Institute of Business Analysis (IIBA) is another certification worth mentioning. Business Analysis Body of Knowledge (BABOK) is the basis reference, which is also published by IIBA. On approximately 250 pages, it describes basic topics of business analysis; for instance, planning of business process analysis, requirement management, enterprise analysis, requirements analysis, assessment of solutions, and competencies of employees. It also provides a comprehensive list of tools such as the SWOT analysis, risk analysis, or various modeling options.

Unlike OCEB, CBAP has initial criteria that require a specific qualification and proof of practical experience.

## Thank You!

Thank you, OMG! The constructive discussion within OMG during the development of the certification program with experts from around the world have ensured a lot of *aha!* experiences. Our special thanks go to Jon Siegel, who runs the OCEB certification program and who did a very detailed review of the English translation of our book.

Thank you, oose! The environment and the freedom that oose Innovative Informatik GmbH give us are very important for our professional and personal further development. Many thanks go to our coworkers and in particular, to Benjamin Kleinow, who supported us actively in the creation of the figures, and to Alexandra Augstin for reviewing the book. Some figures of this book are by courtesy of oose Innovative Informatik GmbH.

Great praise and a big thank you is due to the publisher, dpunkt.verlag, particularly to Christa Preisendanz!

A book can never achieve good quality without a qualified review. A view from the outside is essential.

## Additional References

Homepage about the book: http://www.oceb.de/en

OMG™: http://www.omg.org main page of OMG: http://www.omg.org/oceb, official OCEB page of OMG

Discussion forum of the authors: http://www.xing.de/net/oceb

Direct mail contact: tim.weilkiens@oose.de; christian.weiss@oose.de; andrea.grass@oose.de

Consulting and seminars on BPM: Please contact the authors, tim.weilkiens@oose.de, christian.weiss@oose.de, andrea.grass@oose.de

# CHAPTER 2
# Basic Principles of Business Management

Manager: The man who knows exactly what he cannot do, and finds the right persons to do it for him.

**Philip Rosenthal**

The term *business* is part of the name of the OCEB certification. And as the structure of the certification program already suggests, it is particularly important to the persons behind this idea to establish a common language between experts and IT employees.

This is reason enough to cover the basics of business management and get acquainted with some basic terminology and concepts of this economic science, at least from the business process perspective.[1]

- Business functions, markets, and strategies
- Marketing, added value, and project management
- Costs, efforts, and key figures
- Analysis methods

## BUSINESS FUNCTIONS, MARKETS, AND STRATEGIES[2]

Developing strategies in line with market requirements is not as easy as it seems. This entails some strategic deliberations and careful analyses of the market environment as well as a straightforward consideration of your company's strengths and weaknesses.

---

[1]At this point, we would like to apologize to all business economists: We are well aware that the concepts presented here are not remotely sufficient for discussions even among laymen, but it's a first step.

[2]OCEB reference: Steven Stralser, *MBA in a Day* [32]; Tim Gorman, *The Complete Idiot's Guide to MBA Basics* [16].

## Typical Business Functions

Usually, an enterprise has to do a lot to accomplish its purpose. If you group these tasks very roughly, you obtain business functions that are very similar in most enterprises (Figure 2.1), even if you have the impression that business functions are not departments because a department can execute multiple functions.

In enterprises with traditional organization, however, it is often common practice to establish a department for more or less one particular function. Therefore, *department* and *function* are often used synonymously. In modern and rather process-focused enterprises, however, a function is frequently mapped onto multiple organization units.

Depending on whether a business function directly serves the objective of the enterprise or not, you can distinguish core functions or support functions.

Reflect on Figure 2.1 for a while and particularly note the terms of the functions and the tasks associated with them.

Special attention should be paid to human resources. Apart from the vision of a fully electronic enterprise where only robots work,[3] the employees (and who should know that better than you, dear reader) are the ones that enable an

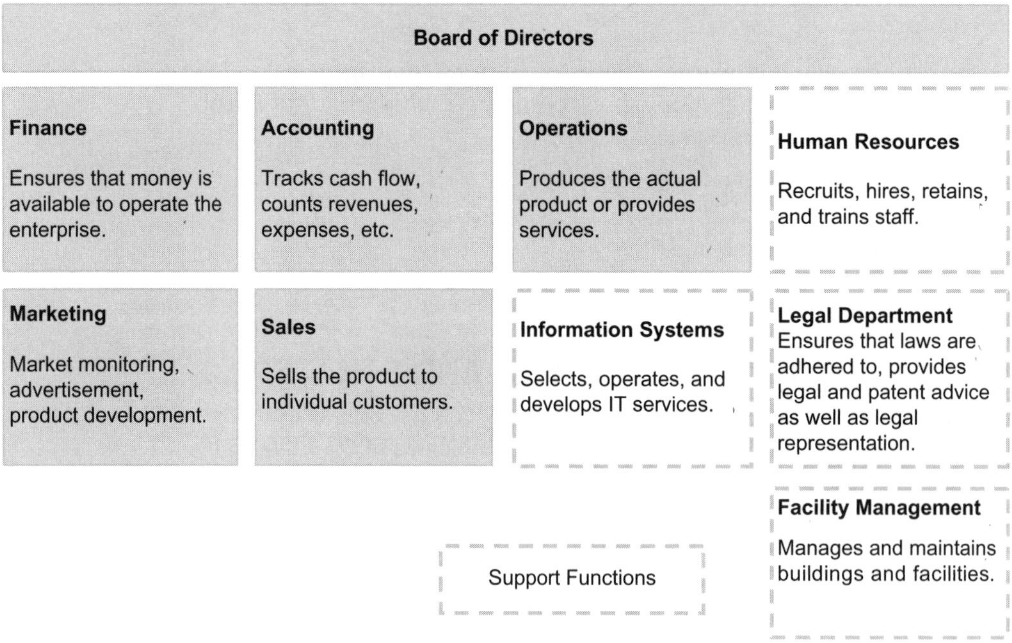

| Board of Directors | | | |
|---|---|---|---|
| **Finance** | **Accounting** | **Operations** | **Human Resources** |
| Ensures that money is available to operate the enterprise. | Tracks cash flow, counts revenues, expenses, etc. | Produces the actual product or provides services. | Recruits, hires, retains, and trains staff. |
| **Marketing** | **Sales** | **Information Systems** | **Legal Department** |
| Market monitoring, advertisement, product development. | Sells the product to individual customers. | Selects, operates, and develops IT services. | Ensures that laws are adhered to, provides legal and patent advice as well as legal representation. |
| | | | **Facility Management** |
| | | Support Functions | Manages and maintains buildings and facilities. |

**FIGURE 2.1**
Typical Business Functions

---

[3]Except for the owner, of course.

enterprise to implement its strategies. Nevertheless, human resources is usually considered to be a support function.

## Managers and Their Competencies

What does a manager actually do all day long? Of course, a certified OCEB cannot answer this question, but he or she knows some basic terms for this.

> **DEFINITION**
>
> The term *management* is kind of old (Latin, *mansionem agere*—the house order) and describes the process of letting things happen by others.
>
> An alternative definition is: "Management is what managers do."

So it's not what is actually organized that's important—the main thing is that others do it.

> **DEFINITION**
>
> A manager is a person who organizes, plans, supports, defines, and assesses the work of others.

If you now look at a complete enterprise, another term is often used in literature, *business administration*.

> **DEFINITION**
>
> Business administration is understood as controlling and organizing business activities.

A manager requires certain key competencies to let wondrous things happen by others. To be more precise, a manager requires seven competencies:

- Goal setting
- Planning
- Decision making
- Delegation
- Support
- Communication
- Controlling

## Business Strategies

Surely, you've played chess before. The goal is kind of clear: win. But what's the best strategy? As you know, there are countless possibilities. Once you've decided on a strategy, you move your chess pieces in compliance with this strategy. You do so until you're convinced that another strategy would be more clever.

This similarly applies to the business strategy. It is always a means to the business end and must match the enterprise's mission (Chapter 5 distinguishes the terms *vision, mission, goal, strategy,* and *tactic* in more detail).

A particular business strategy, as long as it remains valid, defines the direction into which an organization develops. It thus provides a framework for decisions, similar to guardrails on the highway that ensure that all cars are driving in the same direction, at least between two exits.

To acquire an advantage within the changing market environment, it is occasionally necessary to change the strategy in order to newly configure the organization's resources.

## Strategy Development

When a chess player wants to decide on a strategy, he surely doesn't do so without due consideration. Instead, he will gather information, particularly about his opponent. Presumably, he'll take a look at the games of chess the opponent has already played, to determine a pattern and detect strengths and weaknesses.

That's what an enterprise basically does to determine its business strategy:

- First, it analyzes the market environment. (Which forces affect the market? Which factors influence the strategy selection?)
- Then, it divides the market into segments theoretically. (Which buyer groups exist? Are there any market niches?)
- Then, the enterprise analyzes its strengths and weaknesses, if required, for each market segment separately.
- This forms the basis for setting objectives and planning the measures to be taken.

The following discusses the first three items; that is, if you continue reading you get to know some customary techniques to implement these steps.

## Porter's Five Forces

Michael Eugene Porter is one of the leading economists in the area of strategic management and, for many years, he has occupied himself with how enterprises can gain a competitive edge. He developed the Porter's Five Forces framework, which supports an enterprise in selecting a suitable strategy to gain a competitive edge (Figure 2.2).

The idea is simple: The enterprise's success significantly depends on the competitive strategy that is mainly determined by the structure of the market in which the enterprise is active. The market structure of an industry can be attractive or not. But which forces impact this industry structure and thus the attractiveness of a market?

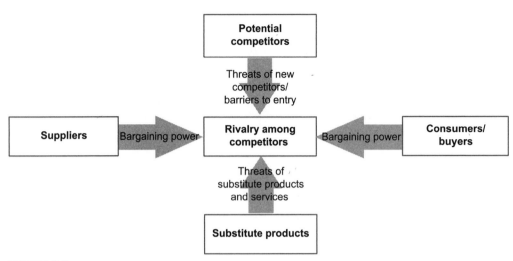

**FIGURE 2.2**
Porter's Five Forces

The following five forces exist:

- Rivalry among competitors
- If an enterprise is already in the market, threats of new competitors, or if it wants to enter an new market, barriers to entry
- Bargaining power of consumers/buyers
- Threats of substitute products or services
- Bargaining power of suppliers

It is obvious that enterprises should attempt to be active in an industry whose market structure is exposed to as few threats of these forces as possible.

## STEP Analysis

Another option to analyze and assess the attractiveness of a market is to use the STEP analysis (Figure 2.3). The acronym consists of the initial letters of the market environment factors to be considered (this technique is also referred to as PEST analysis).[4]

This ready-made system simply provides reference points for considering the opportunities and threats of a market. For example, an enterprise can consider which threats it is exposed to with regard to the trend of interest rates. Likewise, there can be opportunities, for instance, if the enterprise can manufacture products that are subsidized.

---

[4]Different sorting of the terms.

| Sociological/Demographic Factors | Technological Factors |
|---|---|
| ■ Values<br>■ Lifestyle<br>■ Demographic influencers<br>■ Income distribution<br>■ Education<br>■ Population growth<br>■ Safety | ■ Research and development<br>■ New products and processes<br>■ Product lifecycles<br>■ Public research expenditure |
| Economic Factors | Political Factors |
| ■ Economic growth<br>■ Inflation<br>■ Interest rates<br>■ Exchange rates<br>■ Taxation<br>■ Unemployment<br>■ Business cycles<br>■ Availability of resources | ■ Competition with authorities<br>■ Legislation<br>■ Political stability<br>■ Governance principles<br>■ Trade barriers<br>■ Safety directives<br>■ Subsidies |

**FIGURE 2.3**
STEP Analysis

## Market Segmentation

Have you ever been to the Isemarkt in the German Hanseatic City of Hamburg? This is a rather big weekly market that spreads almost half a mile below the city's metro rails. Various market segments, such as jewelry stands, vegetable stands, and so on, are found there.[5] The desirability of the market to a vendor doesn't depend on the whole market, but on the competitive situation in the respective segment.

This does not apply only to weekly markets. For this reason, a complete market for products and services is usually subdivided into small, manageable segments (Figure 2.4). The heterogeneous total quantity of market participants is divided into homogeneous target groups on which market policy efforts should focus.

There are various division strategies for the segmentation of a market:

■ One-dimensional segmentation, for instance, by income classes
■ Multidimensional segmentation, for instance, by countries and income classes
■ Complete segmentation where each customer is handled individually

---

[5]Personally, we (the authors) use the "lunch" segment there, because we work in the vicinity.

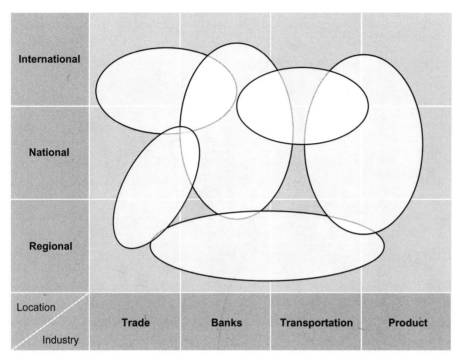

**FIGURE 2.4**
Market Segmentation

Because not every segment entails the same profitability, market niches can arise. They provide an opportunity to gain the leadership in the market segment.

## SWOT Analysis

The previously described techniques (Porter's Five Forces, STEP analysis, and market segmentation) help to analyze the market environment externally; that is, the environment outside an enterprise. It makes you realize which opportunities and threats exist with regard to a market or market segment.

But not only is the market environment of an enterprise of interest, but also the enterprise itself. It has specific characteristics (for instance, quality of products compared to competitors, qualification of employees, level of awareness) with which it acts within the market. Within the scope of an internal analysis, these characteristics can be used to analyze strengths and weaknesses of the enterprise with regard to a market or market segment.

The collected results of the external and internal analysis can be presented initially as an overview using a SWOT matrix (Figure 2.5).

This summarizing comparison often helps you to think about how you can leverage strengths and decrease weaknesses in order to pursue opportunities in a targeted manner and avert threats.

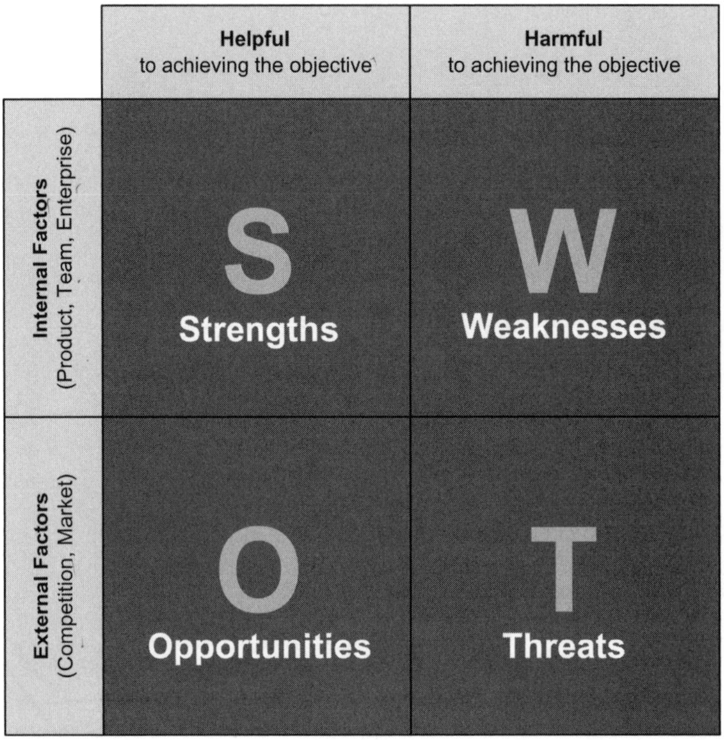

|  | Helpful<br>to achieving the objective | Harmful<br>to achieving the objective |
|---|---|---|
| **Internal Factors**<br>(Product, Team, Enterprise) | **S**<br>**Strengths** | **W**<br>**Weaknesses** |
| **External Factors**<br>(Competition, Market) | **O**<br>**Opportunities** | **T**<br>**Threats** |

**FIGURE 2.5**
SWOT Matrix

When you compare the results of the internal analysis with the result of the external analysis, you obtain four combinations that form a holistic business strategy:

- Strengths + opportunities: Pursue new opportunities that blend well with the strengths of the enterprise.
- Strengths + threats: Leverage strengths to avert threats.
- Weaknesses + opportunities: Decrease weaknesses to leverage new opportunities.
- Weaknesses + threats: Develop defense strategies so that weaknesses don't become the target of threats.

Because each enterprise has both strengths and weaknesses and each market environment involves both opportunities and threats, you should always take all of these combinations into consideration.

## MARKETING, ADDED VALUE, AND PROJECT MANAGEMENT

Marketing is of high significance in virtually every enterprise because the products and services must be delivered to the customer after all.

But why is marketing important for an OCEB? One of the most important business process types is the value chain. It's one of marketing's tasks to design the value chain. Therefore, just like basic knowledge of project management, understanding this term is one of the basic competencies of an OCEB because business process analyses and optimizations are typically handled in projects.

## Marketing

The term *marketing* is not as clear as it seems. A good business process expert should therefore know different uses of this term so that he or she can distinguish them in heated discussions and ask how the others use this term.

A common, rather business-related definition is that marketing describes the orientation of an enterprise in the market.

> **DEFINITION**
>
> *Marketing* is the market-oriented realization of enterprise goals and the alignment of the entire enterprise in the market.

The subsequent advanced and rather economical definition understands marketing as a global event and therefore focuses not only on the individual enterprise but also the interactions in the markets.

> **DEFINITION**
>
> *Marketing* is the process in the economic and social structure that individuals and groups use to meet their requirements and requests by generating, offering, and exchanging products and other things of value.

However you define marketing, you can run "marketing" either reactively or proactively. Consequently, you can distinguish two different forms of marketing (Figure 2.6).

An enterprise uses reactive marketing if it (only) reacts to what others do and responds to them. Proactive marketing, by contrast,

**FIGURE 2.6**
Forms of Marketing

is a philosophy that ensures that resources are deployed in such a way that the requests, requirements, and needs of customers take center stage in the enterprise's activity.

## Process Elements of Marketing

If you understand marketing as a business process (Chapter 3), this inevitably raises the question of which elements or activities this process generally involves.

Marketing is by no means limited to designing brochures and attending trade fairs. This understanding rather involves a very diverse and widespread process that ultimately touches most enterprise areas (Figure 2.7).

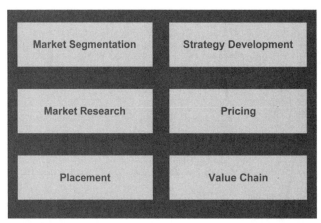

**FIGURE 2.7**
Overview of Process Elements of Marketing

## Value Chain

One term that often comes up in the context of marketing and business processes is *value chain*. Michael E. Porter—whom you already know from Figure 2.2—wrote the following on this topic.

> **DEFINITION**
>
> Every firm is a collection of activities that are performed to design, produce, market, deliver, and support its product. All these activities can be represented in a value chain.

Figure 2.8 shows a typical value chain.

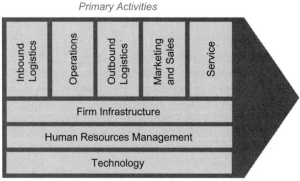

**FIGURE 2.8**
Typical Value Chain

Most notations of value chains typically use arrows to distinguish between core processes (also called primary processes) and supporting processes.

Let's take a closer look at the eight individual elements of the value chain (inbound and outbound logistics, and so on) in Figure 2.8. They are indeed typical, even if you don't find the processes mentioned there in exactly this form in every enterprise or if they have other names.

## Projects

Many plans in the environment of business process management are handled as projects. It is therefore expected from an OCEB that he or she knows what a project actually is. Perhaps you are currently in a project or know from other sources that a project

- Is an undertaking with limited timeframes and budget to deliver clearly defined results, and
- Is undertaken to meet unique goals and objectives.

Great! Then we don't have to write this down now. By the time you encounter certification questions on this topic, you will remember: Projects are limited and unique.

## Project Management

Well, we've already discussed what management is (letting things happen by others, or "what managers do"). Applied to a project, this means the following.

> **DEFINITION**
>
> *Project management* is the application of knowledge, skills, tools, and techniques to a set of activities to meet a specified objective [32].

At first, this sounds trivial. In reality, of course, this process involves a good deal of different tasks, which can be grouped as shown in Figure 2.9.

In this presentation, project management starts with the initiation of the project. The project itself does not start until the project charter has been signed. This is followed by planning, executing, and controlling of the project. Usually, changes arise from controlling so that the cycle starts all over again. The final step of the project is referred to as *closing*.

## COSTS, EFFORTS, AND KEY FIGURES

The basic knowledge of business management naturally also includes costs, efforts, and key figures.

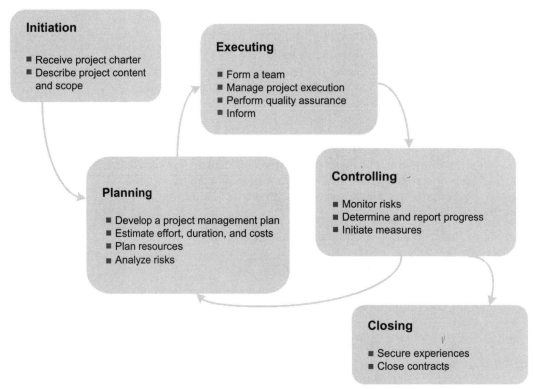

**FIGURE 2.9**
Project Management Tasks

## Cost Types

In the most general sense, you must be able to distinguish between fixed, variable, and overhead costs.

> **DEFINITION**
>
> *Fixed* costs are costs that are constant within a specific period of time and are independent of the production volume or quantity of sales.

Do you have a car? Excellent.[6] Then car taxes and insurance are the essential fixed costs. They incur independent of the mileage, even if you leave your (registered) car in the garage.

> **DEFINITION**
>
> *Variable* costs are costs that vary if the production volume or quantity of sales changes.

---

[6]If not, you can surely use your imagination.

In our car example, these are primarily operating costs, mainly for gas. The more miles you drive, the higher the variable costs are.

> **DEFINITION**
>
> *Overhead costs* are costs that can be allocated only indirectly to a cost unit (product, service).

If you had an entire car pool to rent instead of a single car, then costs for personnel or garages or electricity and water cannot be allocated to a car according to the cost-by-cause principle, but must be distributed to all vehicles.[7]

## Financial Key Figures

Besides the general distinction of cost types there are numerous financial key figures out of which only a few are significant within the scope of the OCEB certification.

But how does an enterprise actually know whether it is able to meet its obligations? This is of central importance at the moment.[8] In principle, it's very simple: It measures the (more or less) available capital.

> **DEFINITION**
>
> Working capital = current assets − current liabilities

First, you determine the current assets. Put simply, these are assets that are available within a relatively short term. These include, of course, not only the money in bank accounts and in cash registers, but also stocks, sellable stocks, and receivables.

To calculate the working capital, you simply subtract the current liabilities from the currently available current assets. The current liabilities include all debts that must or will be cleared within one year. In the best case, an amount that is considerably above zero remains.

When you make an investment—for instance, when you buy machinery—you want to know how cost-effective this is for the capital invested.

> **DEFINITION**
>
> Return on Investment (ROI) = net income/owner's equity

---

[7]You experience this every year when your landlord sends the bill for utility costs, in which the overhead costs are divided among the apartments, taking into account the respective rental areas.
[8]This book was written during the financial crisis in the years 2008 through 2010 when insolvencies of large enterprises and banks abounded.

Let's assume that you invest $10 of owner's equity and use it to generate a net income of $13 after a specific period of time; then the ROI is 0.3. So each dollar you invest becomes $1.30. The greater the ROI the better.

You can use the formula for a single investment as well as for the entire enterprise itself.

## ANALYSIS METHODS

The financial key figures presented in the previous section are all snapshots without any exceptions, which usually refer to a single scenario, for example, to a specific quantity produced.

Reality, however, constantly provides enterprises with a whole series of options. But which one is the best? Business management offers some well-known techniques for this decision making in order to make different scenarios assessable.

### Break-Even Analysis

Let's assume that an enterprise must decide whether to run production in the United States or abroad. The various national markets have different price and cost structures. In other words, the revenues to be obtained on the one hand and the production costs on the other hand differ in the markets under consideration. Which combination of factors is necessary so that the enterprise chooses the United States?

Very simply: It stays if it is more likely to gain profit in the United States than abroad with the same quantity.[9] The quantity where the profit zone begins is referred to as the *break-even point* (Figure 2.10).

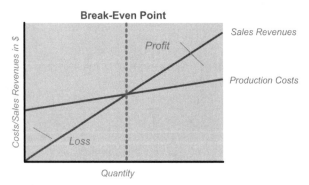

**FIGURE 2.10**
Break-Even Point

---

[9]We beg your pardon: This decision is not that easy, of course. This strong simplification is presented only for clarification, and not to reinforce stereotypes.

Both the gradients and the origins of the two straight lines are usually different. While the sales revenues start at the origin, production costs are incurred, even before production of a single unit. However, the sales revenues have a stronger increase than the costs so that the two straight lines eventually cross at the break-even point. You can calculate this point using the following formula:

$$\text{Break-even point} = \frac{\text{Fixed costs}}{\text{Sales price} - \text{variable unit costs}}$$

If the production costs were identical in both countries, then the enterprise would stay in the country that has a stronger sales revenue line (in other words, the country where higher prices can be reached with identical costs). You can go through the other possible scenarios yourself.

## Crossover Analysis

While the break-even analysis enables the assessment of different scenarios with regard to sales revenues and expenses, the crossover analysis uses the same principle to compare different scenarios with regard to fixed and variable costs. Remember your car? Earlier we briefly used it to describe the difference between fixed costs (taxes, and so on) and variable costs (costs for gas, and so on).

If you only differentiate by costs and are trying to decide whether you want to drive a Porsche Cayenne or Smart, then you don't need a crossover analysis. Compared with Smart, Porsche is clearly superior both with regard to fixed costs and variable costs.

If you want to decide between a diesel-driven and a gasoline-driven car for the same car type, then it's worthwhile to calculate the crossover point (Figure 2.11).

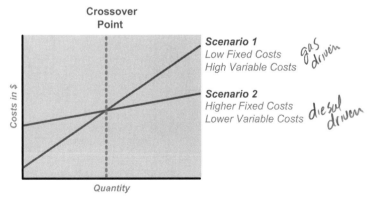

**FIGURE 2.11**
Crossover Point

In Figure 2.11, scenario 2 presents the diesel-driven car. Due to higher acquisition costs, the line starts farther up on the $y$-axis, and its lower gas costs cause a lesser slope of the line. For the gasoline-driven car, the line starts farther down due to lower acquisition costs, and increases more steeply as a result of fewer miles per gallon. The two lines intersect at the crossover point.

In business management, the x-axis usually involves quantities. In this example, however, we don't use the quantity but the annual mileage.[10]

## Decision Trees

Sometimes you simply lose track if you have too many options. Then it is useful if you can visualize the various scenarios to be assessed in a decision tree (Figure 2.12).

The decision tree is somewhat similar to life: You get to a fork in the path and must decide whether to turn left or right (study or earn money?). Then you get to another fork, which may lead to more directions (three different job offers). Every

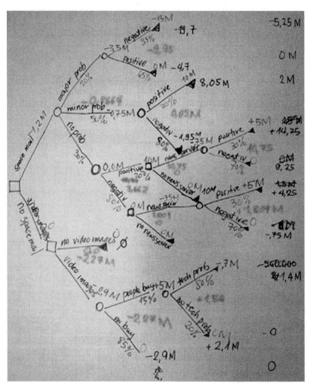

**FIGURE 2.12**
Decision Tree

---

[10]Unless you are a car dealer.

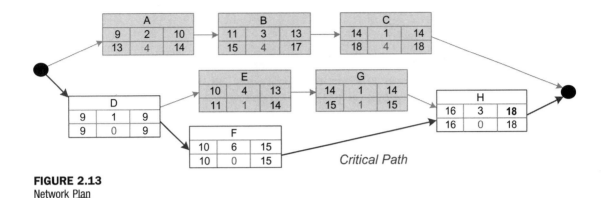

**FIGURE 2.13**
Network Plan

fork is connected with alternative probabilities of occurrence. At the end, you reach the leaves, and you can assess each path by considering the probabilities.

## Scheduling and Resource Planning

Scheduling and resource planning enables you to estimate whether projects can be completed within the timeframe required and whether the required resources are actually available.

One technique available in this context is the network plan where a project is split into individual tasks (A, B, C, etc.) that are then put into sequences (Figure 2.13). Some tasks are independent of each other and can be performed simultaneously. For each task you can specify the earliest and latest start time, their minimum runtime, and the earliest and latest stop time. This information can be used to determine the tasks that have a time buffer and which tasks are on the critical path. If there are any delays on this critical path, this results in delays in the overall project.

## SAMPLE QUESTIONS

Here you can test your knowledge on the business goals topic. Have fun!

You can find the correct answers in Table A.1 of the appendix.

**1.** Which of the following items describe the project management process?
   **a)** negotiate, estimate, budget, report
   **b)** initiation, planning, executing, controlling, closing
   **c)** cost, time, quality, scope
   **d)** plan, do, act, fix
**2.** According to the book *MBA in a Day*, which definition describes the marketing process?
   **a)** Marketing is a process that ensures that brochures and the like are being manufactured in high quality and that arranges the stand at a trade fair.

    **b)** Marketing is a synonym for distribution. Therefore its goal is to bring new products and services to the market and sell them with the highest possible price.

    **c)** Marketing is a social and managerial process by which individuals and groups obtain what they need and want through creating, offering, and exchanging products of value with others.

    **d)** Marketing is the systematization of generating leads (by taking out advertisements on different media channels), evaluating each lead, and then routing them to the sales department.

**3.** Which are elements of an effective marketing strategy?

    **a)** initiation, planning, executing, controlling, closing

    **b)** market segmentation, strategy development, market research, pricing, placement, and value chain

    **c)** inbound logistics, outbound logistics, marketing and sales, service

    **d)** potential competitors, suppliers, consumers, substitute products, and rivalry among competitors

**4.** What is a value chain?

    **a)** It includes inbound logistics, operations, outbound logistics, marketing and sales, service, firm infrastructure, human resources management, and technology.

    **b)** It creates value to the market by considering demographic, technological, economic, and political factors.

    **c)** It is a chain of actions that measure the increasing value of an economic good being manufactured.

    **d)** It describes the performance of a set of company shares. Common examples of value chains are Dow Jones and DAX.

**5.** What is the break-even point?

    **a)** a special item on a Balanced Score Card (BSC)

    **b)** the point at which production costs are equal to the sales revenues

    **c)** the point at which a company becomes insolvent

    **d)** the point at which variable costs overtake the overhead costs

**6.** Which business function is a support function?

    **a)** Sales

    **b)** Human Resources

    **c)** Accounting

    **d)** Project Management

**7.** Which statement about the working capital is correct?

    **a)** It is the company's current assets that are bearing interest.

    **b)** It is the company's liabilities divided by its current assets.

    **c)** It is the limit of amount that can be withdrawn at a cash point within one day.

    **d)** It describes the company's ability to pay its current obligations.

**8.** Which are the main management skills?

    **a)** communication, research, and pricing

**b)** planning, executing, and closing

**c)** goal setting, planning, and controlling

**d)** analyzing, calculating, and facility managing

9. What is the main goal of the business function Finance?

   **a)** to manage financial instruments in order to keep the competitors breathless

   **b)** to ensure that the company has enough money it needs to keep the business running

   **c)** to be informed where the money comes from and where it goes to

   **d)** to decide on expenses, be responsible for mismanagement, and collect bonuses

# CHAPTER 3
# Basic Principles of Business Processes

33

Imagination is more important than knowledge.

**Albert Einstein**

Mainly independent of concrete standards such as the BPMN, this chapter defines and describes business processes in a general way. Topics covered include the following:

- What is a business process?
- Characteristics of a business process
- Discovering business processes
- As-is process versus to-be process
- Levels of business process modeling
- Business processes, goals, and objectives

## WHAT IS A BUSINESS PROCESS?[1]

The general question of what a business process is cannot be answered easily because there is no uniform definition. But, as a matter of course, a certification program on business process management must ask this question. And it is important to have a uniform understanding of the meaning of the term *business process*, not only in the certification program but also in real life. Almost all subsequent concepts are based on it. And if the basis is fragile, many things can go wrong.

But how do we get out of this dilemma? In real life, you should communicate your understanding of a business process and align it with your project team members and other project participants. It is not important how you define the business process, but it is important that all persons involved use the same definition.

---

[1]OCEB reference: Jon Siegel, OMG's OCEB Certification Program, What Is the Definition of Business Process? [28].

The certification program OCEB has not decided on any definition of an author or standard, but created its own paper that describes typical characteristics of a business process and addresses the variety of definitions [28]. This much better reflects the goal of OCEB, to certify business process management knowledge because this variety is part of real life.

One definition is provided by Geary A. Rummler and Alan P. Brache [27], who describe the business process as a series of steps designed to produce a product or service. If the result is directly of benefit for the customer, it is a primary process; otherwise it is a supporting process. Martyn Ould defines business processes as a coherent set of activities carried out by a collaborating group to achieve a goal [26]. The authors Howard Smith and Peter Fingar define the business process in a similar way and supplement characteristics [31]. According to this definition, a business process is complex, distributed, and long running.

The definition of *business process* in standards is similar to the definitions by authors. The glossary of the Workflow Management Coalition (WfMC) describes a business process as a set of one or more linked procedures or activities that collectively realize a business objective or policy goal, normally within the context of an organizational structure defining functional roles and relationships [8]. OMG also has its own opinion on the business process—a defined set of business activities that represent the steps required to achieve a business objective. It includes the flow and use of information and resources[2].

You possibly know many more definitions. But all of these definitions are essentially similar. They describe how an enterprise works. The difference is in the limiting characteristics and the business process's level of detail. For example, the definition of BMM is very general and permits almost all business workflows as a business process. Geary A. Rummler and Alan P. Brache request a customer-related result, and Howard Smith and Peter Fingar characterize business processes as long running. According to some definitions, a business process has a start and an end. According to other definitions, continuous activities, such as risk management, are business processes as well. For real life and for the certification, it is important to know this wide range of definitions.

## CHARACTERISTICS OF A BUSINESS PROCESS[2]

Business processes are complex, according to Howard Smith and Peter Fingar [31]. The characteristic of complexity is often used if things get complicated. There are innumerous discussions on the difference between complex and complicated. If you're interested in this topic, simply browse the Internet. There's a vast number of different opinions on this topic. We'll only examine

---

[2]OCEB reference: James F. Chang, *Business Process Management Systems* [6]; Howard Smith und Peter Fingar, *Business Process Management: The Third Wave* [31]; Laury Verner, *The Challenge of Process Discovery* [34].

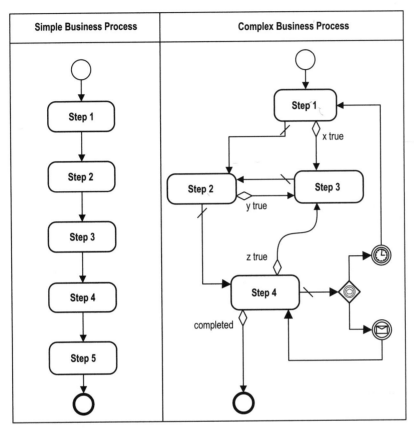

**FIGURE 3.1**
Simple vs. Complex Business Process

which characteristic makes a business process complex. Imagine the process operation in the form of a flowchart, for instance, in BPMN as shown in Figure 3.1.

You can see that it is not the number of steps that makes a process complex. Major, comprehensive processes can be very simple. The number of branches is decisive, which makes the process complex and unclear for the persons involved. This particularly applies if the business process is not documented.

A very important, but not inherent, characteristic of a business process is the ability to be changed easily. Enterprises are subject to constant changes in the market and must adapt to those in a flexible way if they want to be successful in the long term. For example, SpeedyCar only had call centers and some subsidiaries as points of contact for its customers for many years. Market conditions have forced the enterprise to provide its services also via the Internet since the beginning of 2000. Now, additional changes must be made due to the mobile computing trend. Customers surf the web anywhere and anytime via their cell phones and similar devices. This forces the company to implement changed and even completely new business processes.

To ensure that an enterprise can successfully respond to changes in the market, it must continually execute business process management activities. In dynamic markets, a process-focused organization proves itself by responding to change better than a function-focused organization that focuses on departments like finance, customer service, human resources, and so on (Chapter 4). A critical aspect of a process-focused organization is that its business processes are considered and handled as assets within the enterprise (Chapter 4).

Human beings are a central element in the world of processes. They invent processes, execute them, and they are made for them. But processes are not oriented toward individuals, but toward roles; in other words, there is no process that describes the tasks of Tim Weilkiens or Christa Preisendanz. But there are processes describing how Tim in the role of an author of this book cooperates with Christa as the editor. If these roles are assigned to other concrete persons, they follow the same process. The roles work together to fulfill the tasks. The activities cannot be viewed separately by roles. It is the interaction that provides added value. The role of the call center agent is assumed by several persons and the role of the customer (hopefully) by a great many people. The role of the applicant has an abstract character; that is, the role can be assumed by another role, for instance, the customer, which is then occupied by a concrete person.

Another central element of a process involves the process steps; that is, the activities executed by the roles. Besides the sequence of steps, which is determined by the process, business rules must also be adhered to when they are executed. These include, for example, organizational policies and standards. Chapter 7 describes the meaning of these terms.

The explicit process is determined by its topology; that is, by the steps and their interrelations. Flowcharts—created using BPMN, for example (see Chapter 6)— visualize this topology. Figure 3.2 shows the business process, invoice monthly services, as a flowchart in BPMN. Chapter 6 provides some charts that also describe the topic of monthly statements. A good BPMN reading exercise: What are the differences?

The flowchart shows the process topology in the horizontal level. Vertically, you can view the process hierarchy that shows that processes can be part of a superordinate process. Process steps can be described in detail by processes until you come across activities or actions that can no longer be decomposed at the lowest level. Note that the distinction between horizontal and vertical structures also exists for organization units, where it considers another aspect, however (Chapter 4).

For processes, the main focus is often on flowcharts. But there's additional information available for a business process:

- Process owner
- Goals of the business process

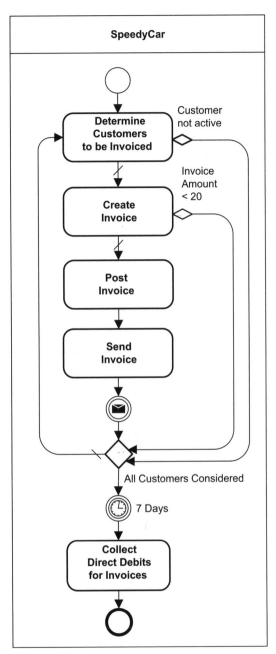

**FIGURE 3.2**
Process Topology in BPMN

- The customer who benefits from the business process
- The stakeholders who can provide important information on the process
- A brief description of the process

The activities—the elementary steps of a process—also have characteristics such as

- Executing role
- Necessary resources
- Data that is required or generated
- Duration
- Business rules that must be taken into account
- A brief description of the activity

As already determined in the previous section, a business process usually is not a random sequence of activities, but a sequence that pursues one or more goals. The term *goal* is a general word whose meaning we want to outline briefly here to avoid misunderstandings.

A goal is a targeted, desirable state. In our context, we consider not only the final goals but also goals (i.e., states) that can also be achieved in the course of the business process. The goal can describe a unique state or can be a steady-state goal, for example, "the complaint rate must be below 0.5% of all bookings."

At least one goal should be assigned to every business process. Start and intermediate states can also be described. It thus becomes apparent how the business processes change the states in the course of time, for example, from the state "customer requests a service" to the state and goal "customer is satisfied."

This information on processes and activities seems to be easy to find and only needs to be written down. In real life, however, this is different. Frequently, knowledge only exists implicitly within the organizations and must be detected first. The next section discusses this topic in detail. The initial recording of business processes is also a undertaking that creates change requirements because the documentation reveals possible weaknesses of the business process. It is therefore also important to distinguish as-is and to-be processes.

## DISCOVERING BUSINESS PROCESSES[3]

Do you have a book in your desk drawer that describes the business processes of your organization? Probably not, and you presumably don't have a corresponding model or document in your IT either. But business

---

[3]OCEB reference: Laury Verner, *The Challenge of Process Discovery* [34].

processes definitely exist, frequently only as implicit, distributed knowledge within the organization. This becomes particularly apparent when staff leave the enterprise taking their knowledge with them. The goal of process discovery is to detect implicit knowledge about as-is processes and make it explicit.

The explicit knowledge of business processes forms the basis for process improvements. You cannot effectively improve or automate processes that you don't know. The supporters of Business Process Reengineering (BPR) object to this statement (Chapter 4). In their opinion, the documentation of as-is processes takes too long and is too incomplete to provide valuable results. It would be more effective to redevelop the business process from scratch. In the 1990s, BPR was hailed as a revolutionary approach and an important drive of the BPM discipline. Since then, it has become viewed more critically.

The purpose of Business Process Analysis (BPA) is to exploit its own process knowledge. It serves to discover weaknesses and enables as-is/to-be comparisons. In his article on process discovery, Laury Verner lists typical examples that require BPA [34]:

- Diagnosing the root cause for a known process problem, such as finding out why the warranty process takes so long
- Finding unknown weaknesses and bottlenecks in existing processes
- Understanding the interrelations and integration of hundreds of data and documents
- Creating standard processes for supply chain interactions, for instance, using SCOR (see Chapter 7)
- Converging multiple parallel processes performed by different departments to a single enterprisewide standard process
- Preparing for measure implementation, specifically to perform an analysis of the new measures on existing processes; for instance, the application of new business rules
- Generating functional requirements for an IT system
- Designing the business logic of a process that will be automated using a commercial Business Process Management Suite product (BPMS)

Discovering and documenting are the first steps in the explicit consideration of the business process. This is followed by the analysis of the as-is process; the process design of a new to-be process that erases the weaknesses of the as-is process; the development of the to-be process; the introduction, implementation, and finally the maintenance of the current process (Figure 3.3).

As described previously, a process also includes roles that execute the process steps. There are three roles involved in process discovery:

- The sponsor who sets up the BPA project assumes responsibility for it and specifies goals
- The Subject Matter Experts (SME) who provide the process content. They frequently come from the management level
- The analysts who control and implement the methodologies of BPA

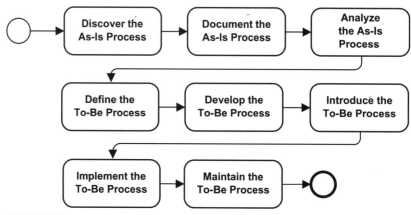

**FIGURE 3.3**
Process of BPA as a BPMN Diagram

Laury Verner differentiates three different ways to approach process discovery [34]:

- **Centralized versus distributed approach**: In the centralized methodology the analyst assembles multiple SMEs together for a series of workshop sessions. This merging of cumulative expert knowledge can lead to positive synergy effects. Predominant SMEs, however, can enforce their opinion toward less dominant persons and thus distort the results. Organizationwise, however, this approach proves difficult because bringing all SMEs together at the same time, particularly if they come from the enterprise's management, is a difficult task.

  The distributed approach is more democratic because the SMEs are interviewed separately by the analyst and consequently all opinions can be handled equally. It is the analyst's task to bring all process fragments together and solve inconsistencies.

- **Top-down versus bottom-up approach**: The top-down approach is the classic method. The analyst starts with an enterprisewide process with a low level of detail; for instance, car rental. He or she identifies the steps of the process and describes each of these steps with a more detailed process, and so on. This approach ensures that the context initially selected is kept. The disadvantage is that process steps that do not fit in the specified hierarchy easily remain undiscovered.

  The bottom-up approach starts with the detailed activities. The SMEs report directly about their work steps. This results in a high level of detail. This advantage is a disadvantage at the same time. The analyst can easily get lost in trivial details. His challenge is to put the various pieces of information in the right context to illustrate the process hierarchy and to determine whether the processes have been identified completely in compliance with the set goal.

- **Structured versus free form approach**: In the structured approach, the SMEs answer predefined questions of the analysts. Ideally, this takes place interactively, but it can also be implemented separately using questionnaires. The structured approaches lead to consistent results. But they can also be incomplete if contents do not comply with the predefined questions.

In the free form approach, the SME reports to the analyst without predefined specifications. The random degrees of freedom allow for the exchange of any information. It is the analyst's task to convert this unstructured information into a structured form.

The three approaches are not mutually exclusive, but are independent. You can take the centralized, top-down, and structured approach or centralized, bottom-up, and free form, and so on.

## DEGREES OF ABSTRACTION OF PROCESS DESCRIPTIONS[4]

You can model business processes at three distinct levels [29]:

- Descriptive modeling
- Analytical modeling
- Executable modeling

The descriptive level maps business processes in a high level of detail. It provides an overview of the process—usually in the best case—and of the organization units and roles involved. Simple diagrams, for instance, using BPMN, or text descriptions can be used for this purpose. The description's goal is to communicate business processes across organization units, for example, to the upper management.

The analytic process description features a considerably higher level of detail. Not only the best case but also the variants and exceptions of the business process are described here. The analyst must have advanced skills in modeling; for instance, workflow patterns, troubleshooting, and handling of events. The result of analytical modeling can be used to analyze the effectiveness of processes. This is also the level of detail that IT departments require to create an implementation that automates the business process completely or in parts.

Executable modeling means that the model itself is executable and can be directly used for automating the business process. This requires a very high level of detail and presents a corresponding challenge to the modeler. BPMN supports the creation of executable models, for example. In real life, however, the modeling tools often differ from the standard and use tool-specific concepts to enable feasibility.

The target group of a business process description is very heterogeneous. Therefore, it is not sufficient to just distinguish the form of presentation. Another view

---

[4]OCEB reference: Bruce Silver, *Three Levels of Process Modeling with BPMN* [29]; BPMN specification [4].

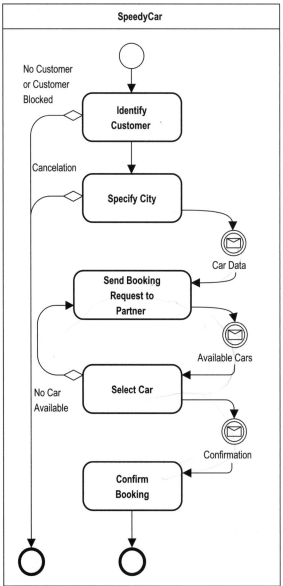

**FIGURE 3.4**
Private Business Process

originates directly from the BPMN specification [4]: private, abstract, and collaboration business processes. Naturally, this differentiation refers to BPMN. However, this view can also be generalized and transferred to other description forms.

Most business processes fall into the category of private business processes.

These are process steps that are executed within the organization only. Figure 3.4 shows the private business process, book car.

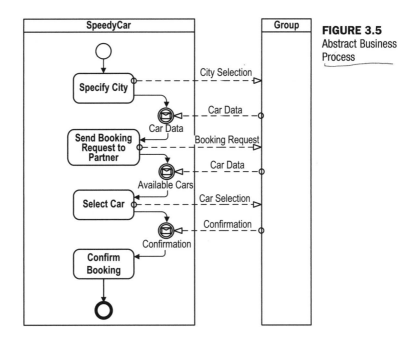

**FIGURE 3.5**
Abstract Business Process

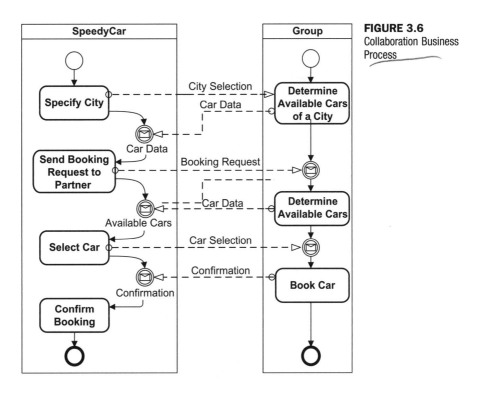

**FIGURE 3.6**
Collaboration Business Process

Abstract business processes describe the interaction between a private business process and one or more of the parties involved. Only those process steps of the private process that are involved in the interaction are illustrated. The process steps of the interaction partners are not described. Figure 3.5 shows the interactions of the private process from Figure 3.4 with the group to be able to book a car of a partner in another city.

A collaboration business process shows an interaction, just like the abstract business processes. However, you can now also include the detailed process steps of the parties involved. The collaboration business process describes the orchestration of the interaction. Figure 3.6 shows the business process of car booking as a collaboration process.

The distinction between private, abstract, and collaboration business processes is independent of the previously described abstractions of descriptive, analytical, and executable modeling. For example, you can model private business processes as analytical or describe abstract business processes.

## SAMPLE QUESTIONS

Here you can test your knowledge on the business process topic. Have fun!

You can find the correct answers in Table A.2 of the appendix.

**1.** According to Rummler and Brache, which is a characteristic of a primary business process?
   **a)** direct value for external customers
   **b)** direct value for stakeholder
   **c)** under control of top level management
   **d)** covers first part of a value chain
**2.** What is a stable and important ability of a business process?
   **a)** complexity
   **b)** transparency
   **c)** changeability
   **d)** documented
**3.** First time documentation of a business process requires which task?
   **a)** consult external experts
   **b)** discover the implicit process
   **c)** define the process
   **d)** evaluate standard process frameworks
**4.** An analyst asks all subject matter experts (SMEs) of a company to send her process descriptions by e-mail. According to Laury Verner, how is this approach classified?
   **a)** centralized, top-down, structured
   **b)** distributed, top-down, structured
   **c)** distributed, bottom-up, free form
   **d)** centralized, bottom-up, structured

**5.** What does a business process diagram show?
   **a)** business rules
   **b)** process topology
   **c)** work procedures
   **d)** process hierarchy
**6.** Which statement describes a process goal?
   **a)** After approval of the request for participation the company sends the acknowledgment and customer card to the customer.
   **b)** The customer must pay the invoices within three weeks.
   **c)** After approval of the request for participation the candidate becomes an activated customer of the car rental company.
   **d)** A customer with no transactions within the past six months will be deactivated.
**7.** What is a typical area of application for a BPA?
   **a)** to establish a new business
   **b)** to detect process bottlenecks
   **c)** to define process roles
   **d)** to analyze the market
**8.** Which level of process modeling is used to provide requirements for an IT implementation of a business process?
   **a)** descriptive modeling
   **b)** software modeling
   **c)** executable modeling
   **d)** analytical modeling

# CHAPTER 4
# Basic Principles of Business Process Management

Continuous improvement is better than delayed perfection.

**Mark Twain**

Just like in Chapter 3, this chapter covers general basic principles rather than concrete standards. Topics include the following:

- Characteristics of process management
- Function-centric versus process-centric organization
- Advancements in process management
- Stakeholders' roles and responsibilities
- Enabling tools of process management

## WHAT IS BUSINESS PROCESS MANAGEMENT?[1]

When you search for the origins of Business Process Management (BPM), you ultimately end up with Adam Smith and his work, *The Wealth of Nations*, written in 1776 [30]. He determined that productivity can be increased considerably by division of labor and specialization. This requires the definition of roles, associated tasks, and a description of how they collaborate. This takes us to explicit business processes, which should be controlled by a management infrastructure. The functional division of labor is still the status quo in many enterprises even today. It leads to a focus on isolated optimization of individual process steps and not on the course of the entire process. Optimization of individual steps, however, does not necessarily optimize the overall process, and may lead to increased costs and undesirable results. On contrast, by viewing the course of the process—from the beginning to the end—we can ensure that optimization helps achieve the process's goals. We discuss this topic in more detail in the next section, which deals with function-focused versus process-focused organization units.

---

[1]OCEB reference: James F. Chang, *Business Process Management Systems* [6].

To find the roots of today's BPM, you typically don't go back to Adam Smith but you usually end up with Total Quality Management (TQM) and Business Process Reengineering (BPR) in the 1980s and 1990s.

The initial ideas of TQM were developed by William Edwards Deming, Joseph Juran, and Kaoru Ishikawa in the 1940s. But it was not until the 1980s that the high market pressure, particularly coming from Japanese enterprises, led to a widespread use of TQM.

It is difficult to define TQM. One of the originators, William Edwards Deming, even said that TQM was only a buzzword, that he never used the term, and that it didn't have any meaning [12]. The fact that he objects to the term TQM doesn't mean of course that he also objects to the concepts of TQM. J. Richard Hackmann and Ruth Wageman provided a sound and acknowledged description of these concepts [20]: According to TQM, the purpose of an organization is to stay in business, so its focus is on preservation so that it can contribute stability to the collective, provide customers with products and services, and offer an environment in which the employees of an organization can develop themselves. The principles of TQM include the following:

- Management by process because quality issues often arise there
- Analysis of process deviations because uncontrolled deviations are the main cause of quality issues
- Quality improvement projects, which should work on a solid data basis about the processes
- Quality improvement, which is a continuous process

The specific techniques of TQM involve:

- Determining customer requirements
- Establishing supplier relationships on a partnership basis
- Setting up cross-functional work groups for quality improvement

In the 1990s, the attention shifted from TQM to Business Process Reengineering (BPR). This shift was initiated by an article by Thomas Davenport and James R. Short [11] and an article by Michael Hammer [22].

The first article suggests a five-level methodology for process revision (Figure 4.1). Two assumptions form the basis of this process:

- IT is a key enabler of BPM.
- Process improvement is oriented toward goals and not toward fixing local bottlenecks and other process weaknesses.

The second article by Michael Hammer was published roughly at the same time. He as well considers IT as a key enabler, but his approach is considerably more radical. Instead of improving existing processes, he proposes to develop them completely from scratch.

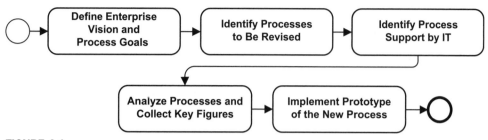

**FIGURE 4.1**
Process Improvement According to Davenport

The goal is to achieve huge progress with regard to cost reduction and quality improvement and not small, incremental steps that take too long overall and thus can jeopardize the existence of the enterprise.

In the reengineered enterprise, everything is aligned with the processes. They, and not the individual tasks, take center stage. Consequently, this leads to a process-focused organization (see the next section).

BPR is described comprehensively in the book, *Reengineering the Corporation: A Manifestation for Business Revolution*, written by Michael Hammer and James Champy [23].

In the mid-1990s—particularly due to TQM and BPR—business process management was labeled as an explicit discipline for the first time. It is a management approach that creates the environment necessary to implement improvement methodologies such as Six Sigma (Chapter 7), TQM, or BPR. The close proximity of these methodologies leads to unclear delimitations, and, as expected, no uniform definition of BPM exists. Instead, there are many principles and practices that characterize BPM. You can find many of these concepts in BPR or TQM.

A rather general, common definition of BPM comes from Mary J. Benner and Michael L. Tushmann [1]: Business process management comprises coordinated tasks to record, improve, and integrate processes of the organization. In this context, the organization is considered as a system of linked processes.

The ultimate goal of BPM was specified by Michael Hammer, who defines it as the improvement of products and services using structured service optimization based on systematic design and management of business processes. Admittedly, this is still very vague and difficult to realize. James F. Chang defines the term BPM in more detail and described four principles and eight tools of BPM for this purpose [6]:

**Principle 1**: Business processes are central assets of the organization to meet customer requirements. It is these assets that create value for the customer and not an individual person or organization unit. The sales and marketing departments of SpeedyCar, for example, cannot render any value for the customers without car service and system development. Therefore, business processes are considered as assets that are directly invested in.

**Principle 2**: As assets, business processes must be managed explicitly. This includes the measuring, monitoring, controlling, and analyzing of business processes, which results in consistent results for the customer and forms the basis for process improvements.

**Principle 3**: Business processes must be improved continuously. It is not a one-time task to implement improvements but a continuous, never-ending task.

**Principle 4**: The use of information technology is essential for the success of BPM. IT delivers information that is required to manage business processes.

The principles are guidelines that lead the way for BPM. The eight tools provide concrete specifications of the tasks to be performed:

**Tool 1**: Establish process-focused organization structures.

**Tool 2**: Nominate process owners. They are responsible for the success of their processes. For this purpose, they must reconcile with the functional units that are affected by the process. SpeedyCar's process owner that is responsible for the car rental process must collaborate with the managers of the functional units, call center, car service, customer support, and accounting, so that the process runs optimally.

**Tool 3**: Upper management must support and promote BPM. The process is improved from bottom to top (bottom-up approach).

**Tool 4**: Establish IT systems to monitor, control, analyze, and improve business processes. IT plays a critical role in the world of business processes. In the 1990s, IT was recognized as a key enabler of process management within the scope of the BPR movement. As a result, IT has moved into the limelight. For example, the revenue of SAP—a provider of Enterprise Resource Planning systems (ERP)—has increased from € 255 million in 1990 to € 7.5 billion in 2001 [6].

Such systems cannot be installed and used easily, but require a tedious adaptation. For this purpose, IT experts must closely collaborate with analysts. The convergence of IT and process management theory is a key concept of process management.

A Business Process Management Suite (BPMS) is a collection of IT applications that supports and measures the business processes [6]. It requires the standardization and linking of business processes. Standardization also involves the integration of data in back-end systems.

**Tool 5**: Collaborate with business partners that are involved in common cross-organizational business processes.

**Tool 6**: Train the employees regularly, and continuously improve the business processes.

**Tool 7**: Combine process improvement with bonus payments and awards.

**Tool 8**: Utilize both incremental process improvement measures such as Six Sigma and more radical approaches such as BPR.

The question arises as to why enterprises should move toward a process-focused organization. The reason can be found in the market that is changing and exerts pressure on the enterprise. Success in the market can no longer be reduced to the simple formula, faster, better, cheaper:

- Faster: The enterprise that launches a product first is successful.
- Better: The enterprise that launches products with higher quality is successful.
- Cheaper: The enterprise that can ultimately offer the products at a lower price is successful.

This formula was valid for a long time. Then, Japanese enterprises, such as Sony and Toyota, emerged that met all three requirements at the same time. This changed market situation has inspired the radical ideas of BPR, among other things. Growing globalization and the associated increase of marketplaces advances the focus on business process management. In their book, Howard Smith and Peter Fingar mention seven trends that illustrate the pressures to which enterprises are subject [31]:

1. The customer is no longer a king, but a dictator. Thanks to the Internet, the customers are well informed and demand what they want.
2. Mass production makes way for mass customization. Dell, which offers customized computers, is a good example.
3. Customers demand holistic solutions. It is no longer just about a single product but also about processes. SpeedyCar not only offers rental cars. The customers can also call on travel agency services such as event bookings or transfers from or to rental offices: a full-service package for all activities that could be related to a drive in the rental car.
4. The boundaries between industries become blurred. Because enterprises offer holistic solutions, they also advance in other industry segments. SpeedyCar, for example, offers some products of the travel industry, such as transfers and hotel booking services.
5. Partnerships instead of competitors. When enterprises advance in other industries, they must also enter partnerships because they cannot meet all requirements by themselves. Successful cooperation with partners requires a sound adaptation of business processes.
6. Value chains are the measure of competition. It's no longer just about who has the best product, but who has the best value chains to be able to offer customers a holistic solution.
7. Change is the only thing that's stable. The rate of change in the market and the associated pressure on enterprises becomes ever shorter and requires more flexible business processes.

# PROCESS-FOCUSED ORGANIZATION[2]

In most cases, organizations have a function-focused structure. This means that the associated functions are bundled in a unit; for instance, accounting, human resources, or customer service. Business processes are orthogonal to this structure. Alignment along functions is also referred to as *vertical structure*, and along the business processes as *horizontal structure* (Figure 4.2). Cross-functional considerations and efficient transfers at the function boundaries are easily forgotten in function-focused organizations. This can lead to inefficient processes despite good functions.

This is exactly where the focus is in process-focused organizations, where the function structure takes a backseat or doesn't exist at all. To successfully coordinate the functions involved in the process is one of the challenges of process management. Concentrating on the horizontal structure may have the disadvantage that functional expertise is duplicated because it is no longer concentrated in the vertical structure.

In his article, "Becoming a Process-Focused Organization" [25], Daniel J. Madison lists several points on culture, concepts, structure, and technique that a process-focused organization should take into account:

> The organization's values must shift from distinction to process excellence. Errors are not considered as errors of individual persons but as an opportunity to improve processes from the insights gained. As an individual person, I can gain a good reputation if I make valuable contributions to more efficient business processes.

The values of the organization enhance the collaboration of the process teams, and standards of the organizations prevent boundaries and territories from forming in the vertical structure. Process owners and department managers must cooperate closely and respect each other. Top management must think in processes and not in functions; in other words, they must map projects onto processes and not onto tasks for the function units.

The organization requires a vision and a mission (see Chapter 5) to provide the necessary context and focus on the business processes. Strategies must directly relate to processes. This can be achieved by using balanced scorecards (see Chapter 7). It should be a requirement to use process-focused methods like Six Sigma, BPR, or TQM.

Shifting from a function-focused to a process-focused organization also affects the structure of the enterprise. It is necessary to create a formal governing body that oversees the organizationwide business processes and sets priorities and provides resources for projects.

---

[2]OCEB reference: Daniel J. Madison, *Becoming a Process-Focused Organization* [25].

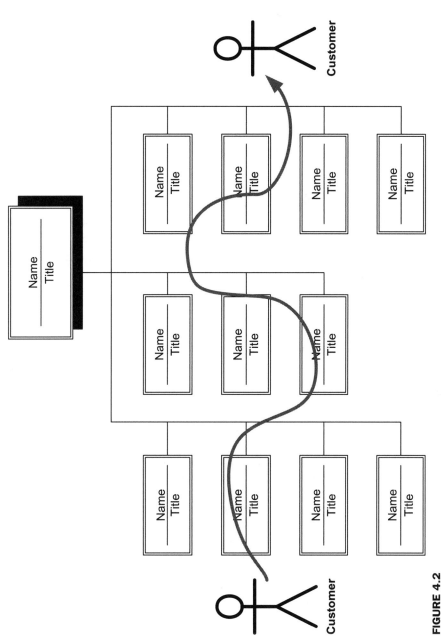

**FIGURE 4.2**
Function-Focused versus Process-Focused

Business processes require a process owner, which may be a new role within the organization. In general, role descriptions should increasingly call for cross-functional abilities to obtain more all-rounders than specialists. Career ladders shift from the vertical to the horizontal structure.

Of course, technology also plays a special role in a process-focused organization. IT must provide the following for business processes:

- Support for modeling and testing
- Full or partial automation
- Provision of information, such as key figures

But good IT alone doesn't result in a process-focused organization; the cultural, conceptual, and structural aspects play a leading role.

## SAMPLE QUESTIONS

Here you can test your knowledge on the business process management topic. Have fun!

You can find the correct answers in Table A.3 of the appendix.

1. Which statement is a business process management principle?
    a) Business processes should be considered for all enterprise decisions.
    b) Business processes should be documented.
    c) Business processes should be automated by a BPMS.
    d) Business processes should be continuously improved.
2. According to Daniel J. Madison what is a strong value in a process-focused organization?
    a) increasing revenue and shareholder values
    b) forming vertical structures to horizontal structures
    c) coordination within and across process teams
    d) automation of business processes
3. What kind of formal governing body is necessary in a process-focused organization?
    a) a body that oversees the enterprise processes
    b) a body that controls the department heads and process owners
    c) a body that specifies IT implementations for process improvements
    d) a body that provides process models and documentation
4. According to James F. Chang, IT is a key-enabler for BPM. For which task is IT important?
    a) Automate processes.
    b) Implement Workflow Management Systems.
    c) Provide process information for the management.
    d) Create process models.

**5.** What is a focus of the process management?
   **a)** shareholders
   **b)** process goals
   **c)** automation
   **d)** quality
**6.** Which approach is associated with an incremental level of process change?
   **a)** BPR
   **b)** BPMM
   **c)** Adam Smith
   **d)** TQM

# CHAPTER 5
# Business Modeling

People who have a vision should go see a doctor.

**Helmut Schmidt**

What do you need to create a model of an enterprise? Right. Pen and paper. But which elements do you want to depict?

The Business Motivation Model (BMM) provides a structure for defining and developing a business plan by describing which purposes an enterprise pursues by which means.

It therefore provides—if you will—a globally uniform vocabulary of rather abstract terms, which often get totally mixed up in common speech. You cannot describe the difference between vision and mission straight away, can you? What about strategy and tactic? Not those either? Alright, then you should continue reading.

## THE BUSINESS MOTIVATION MODEL[1]

The BMM is an OMG standard and describes, on the one hand, the goals of an enterprise with a superior vision and, on the other hand, the associated implementation strategies and tactics with their superior missions.

There is no standardized notation, only abstract syntax. So the BMM only defines the structure and properties of the BMM elements such as vision, goals, and so on, and describes their semantics.

The top-most areas of BMM are the following (Figure 5.1):

- End: Describes the vision of the enterprise and the goals and objectives derived thereof.
- Means: Describes which means the enterprise deploys to meet the enterprise objective. This does not refer to employees or money, but to missions, strategies, and tactics.

---

[1]OCEB reference: *Business Motivation Model Specification* [2]; John Hall, *Overview of OMG Business Motivation Model: Core Concepts* [21].

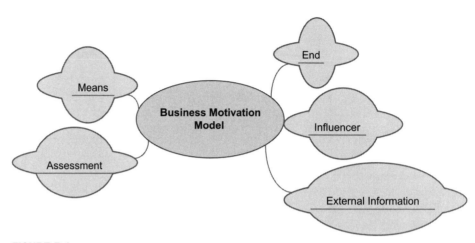

**FIGURE 5.1**
BMM Main Elements

- Influencer: Describes to which influencers the enterprise is exposed; for instance, current market trends, actions of competitors, or internal influencers such as the IT infrastructure.
- Assessment: Assesses neutral influencers on goals and means used; for example, that the Dow Jones collapse in 2008 poses a threat for the enterprise.
- External information: Addresses further important topics of business modeling that are not part of BMM but of other standards; for example, business processes and organization structures. In this area, BMM defines how these topics are incorporated in the BMM.

## Complete BMM Overview

Figure 5.2 shows an overview of the top-most elements of BMM.

The end area is divided into vision and the desired results, which in turn are subdivided into goals and objectives.

The means area is subdivided into missions, courses of action, and directives. The course of action is split into strategies and tactics, and directives into business policies and business rules. The influencers are distinguished by external and internal influencers with reference to the enterprise. The external information[2] comprises organization units, business processes, and business rules. All three information concepts are only referenced here in the BMM and described separately in other OMG standards:

- Organization Structure Metamodel (OSM)
- Business Process Definition Metamodel (BPDM)
- Semantics of Business Vocabulary and Rules (SBVR)

---

[2]Please do not confuse with external influencers.

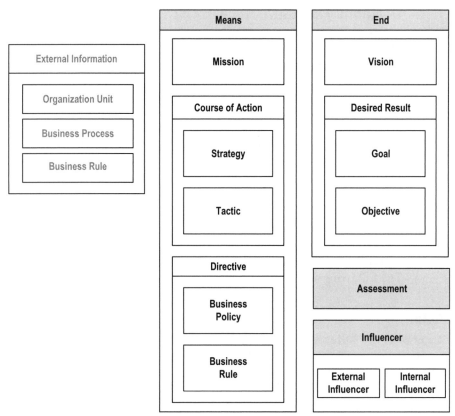

**FIGURE 5.2**
BMM Area (Complete Overview)

Incidentally, all of these are also OMG standards whose usage is not expressly required, but helpful. These referenced standards should be considered representative for the various descriptive forms of these topics. You could just as well describe your business processes with aEPCs[3] instead of using BPMN.

Keep in mind, at the time of this book's completion BPMN version 2.0 will already be present. In the beginning, the BPDM and the BPMN clashed in regards to the development of the BMM. The original BPDM remains up-to-date and has not been edited further. Also, since the test questions are subject to a certain time delay and cannot always reflect the most current information, the substitute symbols for external references remain in-demand for the BPDM.

---

[3]aEPC = aggregated Event-Driven Process Chain

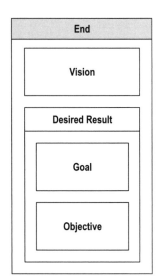

**FIGURE 5.3**
BMM Area End (Overview)

## Scalability of BMM

A business model can become very large and comprehensive. BMM therefore explicitly supports the scalability of very large descriptions in the following three areas:

- Desired result
- Course of action
- Business policy

The elements of these areas can be broken down into subelements using decomposition. For example, you can decompose a goal into subordinate goals that are included in the superordinate goal.

## THE ENTERPRISE'S END

The end area describes the purpose of an enterprise — that is, the vision and the desired result in the form of goals and objectives (Figure 5.3). The following sections take a closer look at these elements.

### Vision

"I spy with my little eye ... a vision." If you apply this typical phrase to an entrepreneur, a vision describes a future image of the enterprise and equally expresses an ultimate, rather impossible, and therefore desirable state; for instance, "We are the leading BPM training enterprise in Europe."

The metamodel (Figure 5.4) is noted in UML (Unified Modeling Language), but don't worry: You don't need a certification in UML for this book. We will explain what you can read from this image.[4]

The right-hand side of the model indicates: A vision includes any number[5] of goals, and every goal amplifies one[6] vision at most. That clearly makes sense: The desire to become a leading enterprise may be a really nice thing. However,

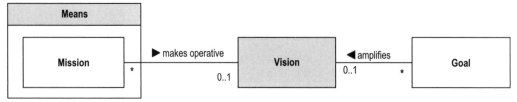

**FIGURE 5.4**
Vision (Metamodel)

---

[4]If you want to learn more about UML, we recommend — completely without any selfish motives — the book "Systems Engineering with SysML/UML" by the same author.
[5]Indicated with the quantity * (meaning: 0 to any number).
[6]Indicated with the quantity 0..1 (meaning: 0 to 1).

you should also be able to derive goals from this desire that ideally are all based on the same vision.

On the left-hand side (read from left to right) the model states: Every mission can make one vision operative at the most. If you read this relation in the opposite direction, it means: Every vision can be made operative by any number of missions.

As mentioned previously, a vision describes a future state of the enterprise. But watch out: In everyday language, the word *vision* is also used to describe desirable states outside the enterprise. You certainly know the following:

> "Our vision is a world where everyone can be connected." — Nokia
> "A PC on every desk in every home." — Microsoft

These are not visions within the meaning of BMM because the BMM vision is supposed to describe an internal view; in other words, it is supposed to refer to the enterprise and not its environment. This car manufacturer, however, got it right:

> "Become the world's leading consumer company for automotive products and services." — Ford

## Goals and Objectives

One single neat image of the future would be too abstract. That is why it is reflected in multiple goals in real life (Figure 5.5). A goal elaborates on the vision; in other words, it describes a long-term goal that must be achieved to amplify the vision; for instance, "Our customers attest that we have very high BPM competency." Hmm ... shouldn't goals be measurable? Right. Something's missing here.

BMM also entails objectives in addition to goals. Every goal can have any number of objectives. An objective has no direct reference to the vision; instead, it can quantify any number of goals—it makes them measurable. Accordingly, an objective is a very concrete, achievable statement with measure of performance — for instance, "At the end of next year, 80% of our regular customers evaluate our BPM competency with 9 or better on a scale of 10."

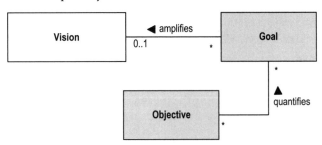

**FIGURE 5.5**
Goals and Objectives (Metamodel)

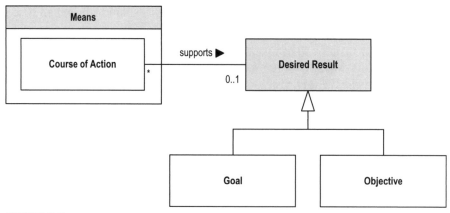

**FIGURE 5.6**
Goals, Objectives, and Means (Metamodel)

## Desired Result

Both goals and objectives describe—speaking abstractly—some kind of desired result. This term is superordinate of any form of goal or objective, so to speak (Figure 5.6).

In the figure, this is indicated with the special form of the arrow, an unfilled triangle, which points from the concrete term to the more abstract superordinate (to be read as "is some kind of" in the direction of the arrow; that is, "a goal is some kind of desired result").

Every desired result of the enterprise (no matter whether it is a goal or objective) can be supported by any number of courses of action. Courses of action include strategies and tactics from the means area, which we'll discuss in the following.

Remember: The end of a business comprises the vision and the desired results in the form of goals and objectives. All of these elements describe a more or less concrete state that the enterprise wants to achieve sometime in the future. Now you know why this BMM area is called *end*.

## MEANS TO AN END

There's a great quote of Joel Barker, a book author, consultant, and futurist, that emphasizes the significance of the means area:

> "Vision without action is a dream. Action without vision is simply passing the time. Action with vision is making a positive difference."

In other words: Visions and goals always imply the means required to implement them. Means can thus be anything that can be used to achieve goals.

Means mainly consist of three elements (Figure 5.7):

- Missions as the counterpart to vision

- Courses of action as the counterpart to desired results
- Directives

In BMM, the means of the enterprise are deliberately described independent of the end. This concept is referred to as *separation of concerns* and allows means to change while the goals remain the same. This makes sense.

## Mission

A mission describes what an enterprise does to achieve a vision (Figure 5.8).

A mission makes an associated vision operative in the first place. There can be any number of missions for a vision — even if Joel Barker, whom we quoted previously, had something different in mind: BMM allows for a vision without missions and also missions without a vision.

Every mission statement consists of three elements:

- An action in the form of a verb; for instance, offer
- A product or service; for instance, training
- A customer or market; for instance, D.A.CH. area[7]

An example for a mission statement would be: "We offer BPM training for enterprises and individuals in D.A.CH."

Unlike the elements from the end area, the elements from the means area don't describe a state (indicated with auxiliary verbs like "be" or "can") but a measure. It is therefore common to word missions according to the pattern "We <make>...."

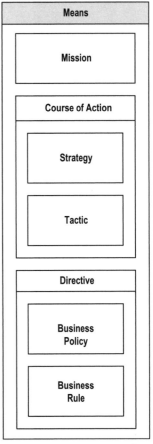

**FIGURE 5.7**
BMM Area Means (Overview)

## Strategy and Tactic

From the previous section you already know that a desired result, that is, a goal or objective, can be supported by any number of courses of action. These courses of action include strategies and tactics.

**FIGURE 5.8**
Mission (Metamodel)

---

[7]D.A.CH stands for the market in Germany (D), Austria (A), and Switzerland (CH).

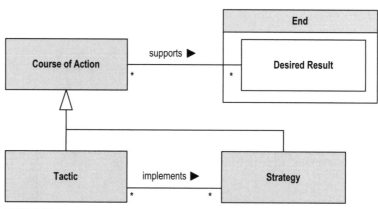

**FIGURE 5.9**
Course of Action (Metamodel)

So you can say that every strategy and every tactic is some kind of course of action and, as such, can support any number of desired results (Figure 5.9).

What exactly is the difference between strategy and tactic? The model indicates that a tactic implements any number of strategies. From this, you can accurately conclude that a tactic already describes a very concrete action while a strategy is still vague.

A strategy, in turn, can be implemented by any number of tactics. BMM considers the strategy to be part of the mission's implementation plan to achieve the goals. The fine print says (please remember): Strategy channels efforts toward goals. Let this sentence melt in your mouth, for it is very important. With this sentence, BMM places the strategy (from the means area) on the same level of abstraction as the goal (from the end area). In fact, it evens requires that a strategy ensures that the "efforts" (= concrete tactics that implement a strategy) are aligned with the goals. This also makes sense.

Let's take the following example:

- Goal: "Our customers attest us a very high BPM competency level."
- Mission: "We offer BPM training for enterprises and individuals in D.A.CH."

Which mission-suitable means are necessary to achieve this goal? The following strategies, for example:

- Strategy 1: "We increasingly publish in the BPM area."
- Strategy 2: "We cooperate with an equally renowned Swiss training enterprise in the BPM area."

We don't know for sure whether these strategies really lead to the desired result. But this gives the direction until you decide on other strategies (that is, change the means).

Tactics for the first strategy could be the following, for example:

- Tactic 1: "Tim, Christian, and Andrea write the first book on the OCEB certification."[8]
- Tactic 2: "Andrea creates webinars and Web Based Training (WBT) for the OCEB certification."
- Tactic 3: "Tim and Christian write an article on OCEB for a professional journal."
- Tactic 4: "We offer preparatory courses on OCEB certification at the OOP conference."

You can see that this is not as unrealistic as it first seemed.

## Business Principles and Business Rules

And because our daily working life doesn't have enough regulatory elements already, there are another two to be considered. The third main element of the means area involves the directive (Figure 5.10).

While the two courses of action, strategy and tactic, only make statements on what is done, a directive describes how it is done. Every directive can govern any number of courses of action and support any number of desired results (goals or objectives). A directive is either a business policy or a business rule.

BMM provides an enforcement level for every business rule. This enforcement level can make a statement on the enforcement of a business rule. The enforcement level can have two characteristics:

- Strict: The business rule must be adhered to. It becomes an organizational procedure (which may be labor law-relevant).

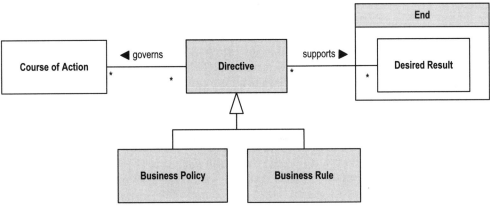

**FIGURE 5.10**
Directive (Metamodel)

---

[8]Which you are holding in your hands right now.

- Guideline: The business rule should be adhered to, but deviations may occur in justified exceptions.

To continue in the previous context, the following would be suitable examples:

- Business policy: "Our ambition is always to exceed the expectations of every customer. Every customer should be positively surprised at least once, ideally with every order."[9]
- Business rule (guideline): "Graphics for publications and training presentations should be created using Visio."
- Business rule (strict): "Employees who are unable to come to work must immediately notify the management stating the reasons and the estimated duration."[10]

## INFLUENCER

Somehow, everything in this world has some kind of influence on something. Tonight's weather forecast will have an influence on the clothes you are going to wear tomorrow. The book you are reading right now will have some (hopefully positive) influence on your everyday work. As you can see, we are gradually encroaching on a philosophical level here.

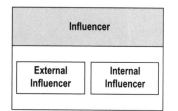

**FIGURE 5.11**
BMM Area Influencer (Overview)

BMM includes these topics, which could be considered part of the humanities. It defines an influencer area that describes to which influencers the enterprise is exposed — for instance, current trends in the market, activities by competitors, or employees' attitude (Figure 5.11). Influencers can be external influencers or internal influencers.

Naming the influencers helps you to understand how and why ends and means of the enterprise have come about. According to this, influencers are concrete events that occurred at a specific point in time, such as the Dow Jones collapse in 2008 during the global financial crisis, or the insolvency of Washington Mutual. But influencers can also involve facts or even habits (unwritten laws), such as, "managers are always recruited from within the organization." The format of an influencer is less important; it is more essential that the influencer is relevant to setting the goal and/or that it has the means to achieve the goal.

Initially, influencers are just there, until someone makes an assessment[11] of how they influence the end and means.

It is therefore important that the influencer itself be described neutrally and not reflect an assessment. As you can see, for every influencer there can be any number of assessments that are considered independent of the influencer (Figure 5.12).

---

[9]Taken from the oose quality policy (http://www.oose.de/ueber-uns/qualitaetspolitik.html).
[10]Take a look at your work contract, where you can surely find a very similar wording.
[11]Assessment is a separate area in BMM, which is discussed in more detail later on.

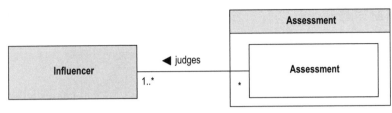

**FIGURE 5.12**
Influencer (Metamodel)

## SWOT Assessment

The BMM's standard procedure for the assessment of influencers is the SWOT analysis, which was already presented in Chapter 2. To do this, you select an (external or internal) influencer—let's say "Dow Jones collapse 2008"—and assess its impact on the enterprise. For many enterprises, the impact may pose a threat; others conclude that it provides a great opportunity. The assessment may lead to a new goal for which you must find suitable means for implementation. The next section provides more information on this.

## External and Internal Influencers

An enterprise is exposed to influences from the outside or from within. For this reason, BMM makes a distinction between external and internal influencers. Every influencer can be assigned to different categories. The BMM has already defined default categories for external and internal influencers (Tables 5.1 and 5.2). You can add further categories if you want.

An example for an external influencer (category: competitors) would be: "Two competitors have merged and are therefore larger than the enterprise considered."

A concrete example for an internal influencer (category: privilege) would be: "The management has decided that, in the next three years, expansion in Switzerland has priority over other countries."

| **Table 5.1** | **Default Categories for External Influencers** |
|---|---|
| Competitors | Environment |
| Customers | Regulation, laws |
| Partners | Technologies |
| Vendors | |

| **Table 5.2** | **Default Categories for Internal Influencers** |
|---|---|
| Assumption | Point of issue |
| Enterprise value (implicit, explicit) | (Management) privilege |
| Habit | Resource, supplies |
| Infrastructure | |

## ASSESSMENTS

Have you ever been to an assessment center? If not, imagine a row of judges (maybe from sports) who hold up their marks after you've given your presentation. They "assess" you.

This is exactly what happens to an influencer, which is a neutral element initially. The influencer is not evaluated until the assessment. More precisely: The assessment judges the impacts of the influencer on the end or the means of the enterprise. The overview of this separate area is rather plain; it contains only one single element, shown in Figure 5.13.

Assessment

**FIGURE 5.13**
BMM Area Assessment

This area is not particularly comprehensive; however, the assessment establishes the logical link between the influencers and the end and means of the enterprise. The metamodel illustrates this (Figure 5.14).

An assessment can judge multiple influencers (but at least one). This makes sense because otherwise you wouldn't know what the assessment refers to. In this context, it doesn't matter whether the influencer is external or internal.

It is possible that the assessment affects achievement of any elements from the end area; for instance, goals or objectives or even the vision. In the previous model, the term *end* is used as a superordinate for these elements.

And finally, the assessment can affect the employment of any means—in other words, it can lead to new missions, strategies, tactics, policies, or business rules. Here again, means is to be understood as a superordinate for these things.

SWOT assessment—again? Déjà vu? That's right. So that SWOT really haunts you in your dreams, the following illustrates the topic from another perspective: Every assessment can be provided with different categories. If you cannot think of anything new, simply use one of the SWOT letters for strength, weakness, opportunity, or threat as the default assessment category—that's what the BMM suggests.

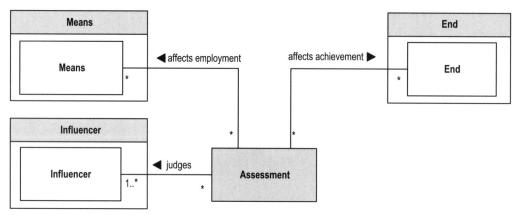

**FIGURE 5.14**
BMM Area Assessment

Typically, there's a context relationship between the type of influencer (external or internal) and the SWOT categorization of an assessment. Although this is self-evident, it is helpful to call attention to this fact: Presumably, you would assess the Dow Jones collapse neither as a strength nor as a weakness, but only as an opportunity or threat. Got the context? Exactly: External influencers are categorized as opportunities or threats, while internal influencers are assessed as strengths or weaknesses.

## ORGANIZATION UNIT

Imagine that you (for whatever reason) modeled an enterprise's vision, the most essential goals and objectives such as missions, strategies, tactics, business policies, business rules, influencers, and even their assessments, and everything just looks great: Well, congratulations!

But what's the use of this model if you don't specify who is to execute the tactics and business processes or comply with the business rules? This directly takes us to the department or the general organization unit (Figure 5.15).

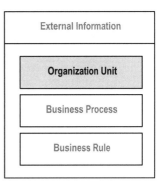

The organization units are part of the external information, just like business processes and business rules. Well, at least from the BMM perspective. Here, OMG clearly delimits the BMM from other standards and, in the BMM, provides placeholders for other standard concepts.

So it is the task of another standard, for instance, the Organization Structure Metamodel (OSM), to describe the organization units. But the BMM defines how organization units should be linked with the BMM elements. Accordingly, concrete logical links of BMM and organization units are as follows. An organization unit

**FIGURE 5.15**
BMM Area Organization Unit

- Defines ends
- Establishes means
- Recognizes influencers
- Makes assessments
- Defines strategies
- Is responsible for business processes

Business can be so easy.

## LEVELS OF ABSTRACTION IN MODELING

Have you ever been to the Miniatur Wunderland in Hamburg? If not, you may have read about it in various travel guides. There, various scenes and gigantic landscapes are recreated in model railroad format across multiple floors; everything is built with an absolutely unbelievable love for detail. A beautiful example for models as copies of reality.

BMM is also about models—enterprise models. This being the case, it is obvious that the OCEB certification program also deals with the rather general topic of abstraction levels in modeling.

## The Art of Abstraction

In the Miniatur Wunderland, you don't see all details of reality, which is a good thing, because abstractions are necessary to structure complex situations and reduce them to a manageable and comprehensible dimension. Otherwise, you would be overwhelmed by the flood of information.

Comprehensive situations are ideally mapped at different levels of abstraction, where each abstraction level should represent a meaningful view of reality so that it can be communicated easily. Unfortunately, you cannot measure the degree of abstraction, but human beings are able to compare two elements and tell which one is more concrete than the other. This is basically enough to ensure to a certain extent that elements of the same degree of abstraction are at the same level of abstraction.

An example for levels of abstraction would be the levels of business processes, business workflows, and business scenarios (Figure 5.16). A business process consists of multiple courses of business and a scenario is a concrete business workflow.

So if Sam Shark calls SpeedyCar to rent a car for the next day, this is a business scenario. The business workflow, however, describes in general[12] how a new car booking is made. A business process additionally describes business workflows such as changes, cancellations, and billing of car bookings.

The more you abstract (go to higher levels), the more details you must omit. And still the abstraction is able to add value; that is, it only makes sense if it is still concrete enough. In other words (if you are still looking for quotes): "Good modeling is the art of getting concrete at an abstract level" (Tim Weilkiens [36]).

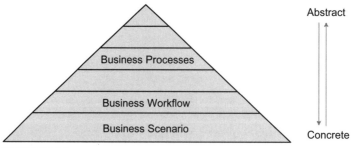

**FIGURE 5.16**
Abstraction Hierarchies

---

[12]We could almost used the word "abstractly" here.

At the highest levels of abstraction, the added value mainly consists of the overall view. This involves those nice maps that can be found in many enterprises and are often used to get started. Even if such "abstract" overviews appear rather trivial, their development definitely wasn't. And as a structural graphic, a highly abstract model may look neat and tidy.

## Static and Dynamic Models

Whatever topic you select: Start modeling at an abstraction level where modeling seems to be easy. You can use this as the basis for detailing.

The outcome of this decomposition also depends on the type of model. Static models map a specific structure. The human skeleton is a good example here: head, upper limbs, body, and lower limbs. The lower limbs include upper leg, lower leg, foot, and so on. As you can see, you can easily dissect a skeleton—in your imagination at least.

In dynamic models, it's not that easy because their elements are structured in a network and not in a hierarchy as in business workflows, for example. In this context, the abstraction levels may play an important role, because they can help notionally retrieve elements within those networks.

Business modeling creates mainly static models, while the modeling of business processes focuses primarily on dynamic models. Then the dynamics is much more interesting than the structural context, particularly if it involves cross-organizational aspects. Business process models therefore illustrate mainly activities of people, decisions, and the collaboration of departments.

## Systems Thinking[13]

In the upper levels of abstraction, you are quickly confronted with the topic of systems thinking. Systems thinking means to consider the system as a whole. All parts, their connections, and interactions are taken into account. The traditional analysis (Greek *analysis* = a breaking up) breaks up a system into its individual parts and runs an isolated inspection. Systems thinking helps master complexity.

You surely have used Google Earth to search for your home, right? Starting in space, you first zoom to your continent, then to your country, and so on until you can see your house (and find out, to your own horror, that the recording was made last Sunday because you can see the car of your in-laws).

What's the reason for this excursion? It wants to illustrate: Everything is a system.[14] When you hear the term *system*, you quickly think of technical systems. But that is not what is meant here. Everything that you can perceive as a unit

---

[13]OCEB reference: Peter Fingar, *Systems Thinking: The "Core" Core Competency for BPM* [14].

[14]"Everything is an object" comes from Alan Kay, Dan Ingalls, and Adele Goldberg, developers of the object-oriented programming language SMALLTALK. Today, we're one step ahead.

of structures and interactive elements constitutes a system. The earth is a system. The United States is a system. And even your family in your house is sort of a system.

In terms of business process management, systems thinking constitutes the top-most level of abstraction. The enterprise is a system, and the processes are its elements, which in turn include business workflows and these again, business scenarios.

Organization units, resources, and other things are also integral parts. Systems thinking is supposed to consider all elements and their interactions.

## Syntax, Notation, and Semantics

In order to model systems, you require a modeling language consisting of syntax (vocabulary of the language including notation and grammar — i.e., including rules on how to use the vocabulary) and semantics (the meaning).

The syntax can be subdivided into concrete and abstract syntax:

- The *concrete syntax* is the (usually graphical) visualization of vocabulary, which is also referred to as *notation*. For example, you can consider whether you want to illustrate the vision as an eye and a goal as the bull's-eye of a target.
- The *abstract syntax*, by contrast, involves a defined vocabulary (vision, goal, and so on) and its structural context. In BMM, this abstract syntax is defined as UML models.

Abstract and concrete syntax ultimately specify how an enterprise model can be described with concrete elements, for example, the defined vision and concrete goals and objectives. The BMM specification therefore contains a model of an enterprise model (hence the root word "meta"). As mentioned initially, the BMM does not define any notation (concrete syntax), but leaves it up to you to select the appropriate notations (Figure 5.17).

So if you want to use BMM in real life, you must design your own graphical notation (sign language). Compared with pure text documentations, graphical models have the following benefits:

- Graphics can be understood and memorized faster.
- A specific perspective of reality can be presented in a targeted manner.
- An existing metamodel already provides a meaning for the concrete model, without having to document it explicitly once again.

Semantics describes the meaning and the use of the model element, if required.

With regard to the vision, the BMM says: "A Vision describes the future state of the enterprise, without regard to how it is to be achieved [...]." This meaning helps us to find the right level of abstraction.

Precisely because a model is always an abstraction, it should always be unambiguous. Well-defined syntax and semantics provide support here. The more

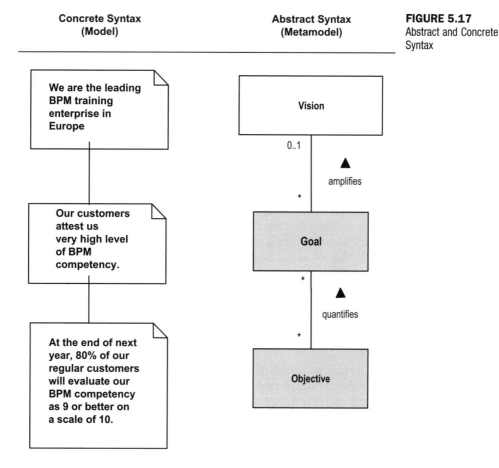

Concrete Syntax (Model)     Abstract Syntax (Metamodel)

**FIGURE 5.17**
Abstract and Concrete Syntax

unambiguously you define abstract syntax, notation, and semantics, the sooner different users obtain a common, and, above all, holistic understanding of a model's meaning. Therefore, specifications such as BMM try to illustrate situations with many graphical UML models and combine them skillfully with natural language.

## SAMPLE QUESTIONS

Here you can test your knowledge on the business modeling topic. Have fun! You can find the correct answers in Table A.4 of the appendix.

1. A car rental company plans to open new branches in other countries. Which BMM element must be used to describe that statement?
   a) goal
   b) mission
   c) strategy
   d) vision

**2.** A car rental company plans to double the number of customers within the next five years. Which BMM element must be used to describe that statement?
   **a)** goal
   **b)** vision
   **c)** strategy
   **d)** objective

**3.** Which aspect fits best to the systems thinking discipline?
   **a)** product development and operation
   **b)** abstraction and complexity
   **c)** communication and presentation
   **d)** simulation and optimization

**4.** What is most important about the semantics of a model element?
   **a)** It has only one meaning.
   **b)** The meaning is commonly accepted.
   **c)** The meaning is concrete.
   **d)** The meaning is abstract.

**5.** Which are elements of a modeling language?
   **a)** abstract syntax, concrete syntax, semantics
   **b)** notation, semantics
   **c)** vocabulary, grammar, relationships
   **d)** syntax, concrete semantics, notation

**6.** The annual report of a car rental company shows that there is an increasing demand for luxury cars. Which BMM element must be used to describe that statement?
   **a)** tactic
   **b)** assessment
   **c)** influencer
   **d)** opportunity

**7.** For the first time a car rental company is fair according to slight car damages like minor scratches. Which BMM element must be used to describe that statement?
   **a)** business policy
   **b)** strategy
   **c)** tactic
   **d)** mission

**8.** What are top level elements of the end area?
   **a)** mission, course of action, directive
   **b)** vision, desired result
   **c)** business rules, business processes, organization unit
   **d)** assessment, influencer

**9.** How could a competitor be described in BMM?
   **a)** threat
   **b)** actor
   **c)** influencer
   **d)** market

**10.** Which concept does BMM use to enable large models?
   **a)** separation of concerns
   **b)** decomposition
   **c)** abstraction
   **d)** packaging
**11.** What is a set of categories for an assessment?
   **a)** SWOT
   **b)** external, internal
   **c)** end, means
   **d)** rule, policy, procedure

# CHAPTER 6
# Modeling Business Processes Using BPMN

The most pleasant thing is to get what you want.

**Bruno Snell**

In the OCEB Fundamental exam, 40% of all questions refer to the BPMN. These questions are divided into the following areas:

Modeling concepts (24%):

- What is BPMN?
- Diagram elements
- Sequence flows
- Activities and decompositions
- Events
- Gateways
- Data objects, artifacts, and associations
- Message flows
- Groups
- Differences between parallel and sequential flows

Modeling skills (16%):

- Pools and lanes
- Activities and subprocesses
- Gateways: OR versus AND versus XOR (exclusive, parallel, and inclusive gateway)
- Start and end events
- Intermediate events (for instance, timer)

This examination typically tests definitions, symbols, and syntax of the BPMN. Moreover, it uses concrete examples to examine the extent to which the reader understands the content of the diagram.

## WHO OR WHAT IS BPMN?[1]

If you take a look at the current notations for business process modeling, you find three main notations: the EPCs (Event-Driven Process Chains), UML (Unified Modeling Language[2]), and, more recently, BPMN (Business Process Modeling Notation[3]).

Do you already create models using BPMN or do want to use it in the near future? Then the OCEB certification is available at exactly the right time.

But before we start detailing the BPMN, let's take a look at its short history.

In 2002, Stephan A. White developed an early version of the current BPMN in co-operation with the BPMI (Business Process Management Initiative). Since 2006, BPMN has been an international standard of OMG. The OCEB examination is based on BPMN Version 1.1, which was adopted by OMG in 2008. Currently, BPMN Version 2.0 is being processed through the steps that will make it an OMG standard.

### Goals of BPMN

BPMN was defined to achieve the following goals:

- Provide a standardized graphical notation for modeling business processes.
- The notation can be understood by all stakeholders, from business analyst to process implementer.
- The notation can also be mapped to executable XML-based process languages (such as Business Process Execution Language for Web Services, BPEL4WS[4]).

If you sneak a peek at the specification,[5] it provides you with all elements of the graphical notation and a mapping of BPMN to BPEL4WS (see Appendix).

BPMN 1.x supports one single diagram type only: the Business Process Diagram (BPD). The BPD includes an image of the business processes. For this reason, the focus of the BPMN is not on the following:

- Organization structure
- Resource structure
- Data and information models
- Business strategies and business rules
- Definition of an exchange format like BPEL4WS[6]
- Metamodel[7]

The next section introduces you to BPMN using an example.

---

[1]OCEB reference: Business Process Modeling Notation (BPMN) [4].
[2]A standard of OMG that is highly prevalent in the IT environment.
[3]As of the new version BPMN 2.0, the abbreviation stands for Business Model and Notation.
[4]BPEL4WS is an XML-based language for describing business processes whose individual activities are implemented via web services.
[5]Download at http://www.bpmn.org.
[6]Only a mapping to BPEL4WS is defined and not the language itself.
[7]A metamodel is available as of BPMN 2.0.

# IN A NUTSHELL: AN INTRODUCTION TO BPMN

BPMN claims to be easy to understand—we will use an example to convey the basic concepts of BPMN, so you can see for yourself if this is true. Then you can go directly to the details. A BPD consists of activities, events, and gateways, which a sequence flow puts in a flow sequence. Activities, events, and gateways are summarized under the term *flow object*.

Figure 6.1 describes in BPMN how the car rental company SpeedyCar creates a monthly statement for a customer that includes all of the customer's rentals.

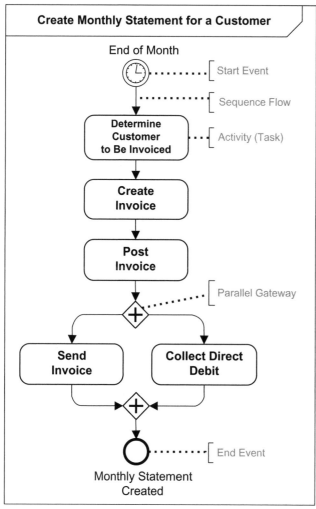

**FIGURE 6.1**
Monthly Statement

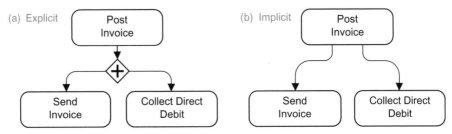

**FIGURE 6.2**
Branching in Parallel Workflows

In order to name the individual BPMN elements in the diagram, we used a lot of comments. Comments are indicated with an open square bracket in BPMN and can be linked with other model elements using a broken line, the association.

The start event marks the start point of a flow. Events in BPMN can have a type that indicates the circumstances under which an event occurs, the trigger. In this example, the process starts with the start event end of month of the timer type. As soon as the end of the month is reached, the incoming event starts the process, Create monthly statement for a customer.

A time event is triggered at a concrete point in time—for example, 08/02/2008, 02:08 A.M.—or by a recurring time event—for example, at the end of the month. Message is another event type. For example, an incoming phone call or an incoming e-mail of the message type can start a process.

As soon as a process is called, the start event receives a token. A token is a kind of virtual marble that rolls through the process and thus simulates the workflow. Unlike a real marble, the token can proliferate or be destroyed. The process ends when the last token is resolved.

In Figure 6.1, the token runs from the start event to the tasks Determine customer to be invoiced, Create invoice, and Post invoice, via the sequence flow. After the post invoice task, the sequence flow enters a parallel gateway. The gateway splits the sequence flow into two parallel lines, which doubles the token. Each sequence flow receives a token.

BPMN offers two options to illustrate parallel flows: explicit using a parallel gateway or implicit using several sequence flows that leave an activity. In both cases, each outbound sequence flow receives a token and both tasks Send invoice and Collect direct debit are triggered (see Figure 6.2).

**FIGURE 6.3**
Joining Parallel Flows

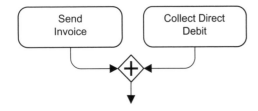

The parallel gateway can split or synchronize parallel workflows. In the synchronization, several sequence flows lead into the gateway and only one leads out (see Figure 6.3). The gateway waits until a token is available at every incoming flow. Only then are the tokens joined, and the flow continues.

In this example, the parallel activities Send invoice and Collect direct debit are synchronized in a parallel gateway. Only when the two tasks have been completed does the flow continue.

In Figure 6.1, the token then proceeds to an end event, which marks the end of the process and destroys exactly one token. Because no other token is active, the Create monthly statement for a customer process is completed.

Now, let's enhance the process: In addition to direct debit payment, we will also enable credit card payment (see Figure 6.4).

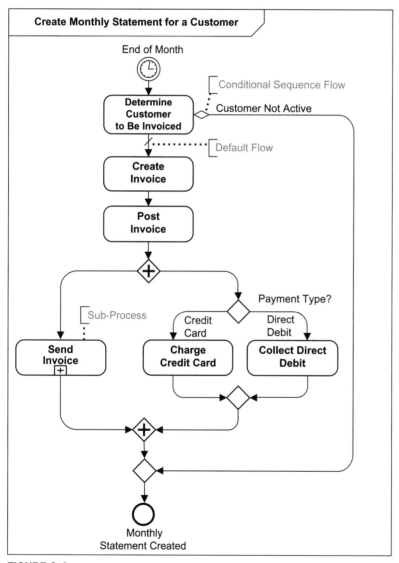

**FIGURE 6.4**
Monthly Statement

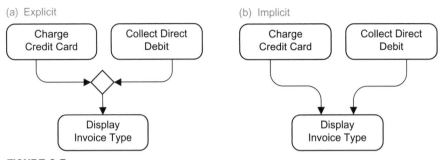

**FIGURE 6.5**
Merging Alternative Flows

In order to express that exactly one alternative can be selected, we use exclusive gateway. Either the customer pays with a credit card or pays via debit, but not with both.

In an exclusive gateway, the token runs along the sequence flow whose condition is met first. As the name of the gateway already suggests, exactly one sequence flow is selected exclusively.

After Collect direct debit or Charge credit card, the sequence flow is merged with an exclusive gateway again. As soon as one of the two tasks is completed, the token migrates to the gateway and passes it without any delay.

As an alternative to the exclusive gateway, the sequence flow can also be merged in an activity. If several sequence flows end in a single activity, each incoming token triggers the activity.

For example, as soon as Collect direct debit or Charge credit card has been executed, the Display invoice type activity starts (see Figure 6.5).

Instead of using the exclusive gateway, you can also model this behavior using conditional sequence flow. It is diagrammed with a small diamond directly at the activity. The behavior of the two notations is identical if associated conditions are mutually exclusive. For example, if the customer requests an e-mail delivery, the Create e-mail with invoice activity is executed (see Figure 6.6).

**FIGURE 6.6**
Conditional Sequence
Flow

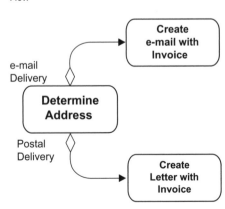

However, if several conditions are true, all associated sequence flows receive a token. Thus flow may be parallelized, depending on the conditions. This would be the case if the customer has selected e-mail delivery and postal delivery.

In case of an exclusive gateway or a conditional sequence flow, you can specify a default flow. It receives a token if none of the conditions specified is true. You can use a default flow to prevent the flow from stopping if one of the required conditions is valid (see Figure 6.7).

In order to avoid having to model a complex process across entire walls (in the literal sense), you can divide a process into

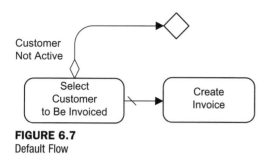

**FIGURE 6.7**
Default Flow

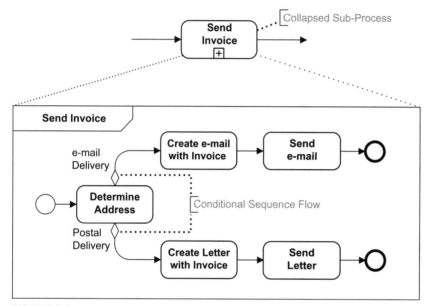

**FIGURE 6.8**
Subprocess with Detailing

several processes. In Figure 6.8, Send invoice is shown as a subprocess. The "+" sign indicates that the detailing of Send invoice was transferred to a separate diagram.

Processes and business objects are closely intermeshed in business processes. A process works with business objects; that is, it can create, change, or destroy them. In BPMN, business objects are modeled as data objects and have no influence on the sequence flow.

In Figure 6.9, the invoice data object has an association with the create invoice activity. The nondirectional association does not specify whether the invoice flows in or out of the activity.

This is different in the second example: If the invoice data object has the created state, it is included in the Send invoice activity, which is indicated with a directional association. The activity changes the data object by setting the state to Sent.

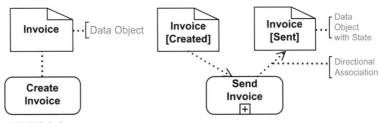

**FIGURE 6.9**
Examples of Data Object

Business processes often involve participants. Pools are used to subdivide a process according to the different organizations that participate. Examples include customers, enterprises, or suppliers. Figure 6.10, Process Damage Report, includes three pools: driver, SpeedyCar, and the person responsible for booking. If the flow within a pool is not relevant, the pool can be displayed as a black box—as for the person responsible for booking. The internal flow is hidden in this case.

Each pool is responsible for its own process and can communicate with other pools via message flows. The driver sends SpeedyCar a damage report message. The incoming message starts the process in the SpeedyCar pool.

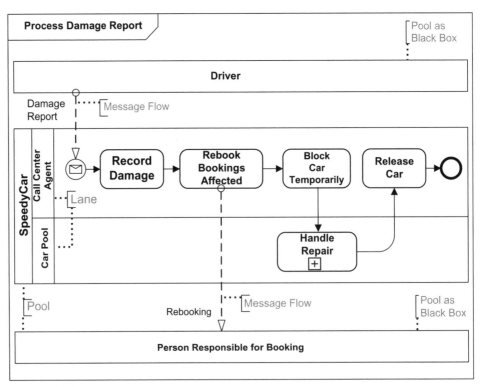

**FIGURE 6.10**
Process Damage Report

With lanes, you can structure an organization in different ways; for example, by groups or roles. In this example, SpeedyCar includes the car pool and call center agent lanes. Lanes communicate with other lanes within the same pool using sequence flows.

Our brief introductory example is complete. Let's now go into the depths of BPMN.

# TOKEN

A process models flow scenarios that can be simulated and illustrated using tokens. Moreover, the exact rules of BPMN elements can be described well using the token semantics.

Think of a token as a sort of virtual marble, which is generated when a process is called and represents the process flow along events, activities, gateways, and sequence flows. A token never crosses the message flow to reach the flow of another pool. No graphical symbol is defined for the token in the BPMN specification. To illustrate flow scenarios and describe special BPMN elements, we picked a symbol to represent our virtual marble in this book.

The token with number 3.2 is the second token at time 3 (see Figure 6.11).

Figures 6.12 through 6.18 show the concrete flow of the marbles through a process at different points in time in flip-book style.

When a process begins, the start event generates a token as shown in Figure 6.12. The token migrates to the first activity along the sequence flow. Whenever a token touches an activity, that activity is executed.

After the activity has been processed, the token goes to the next flow object via the sequence flow (Figure 6.13).

There, it encounters a gateway. Depending on the gateway type, the token exhibits different behavior. Because this is a parallel gateway, the token is cloned so that all parallel branches receive a token (Figure 6.14).

3.2

**FIGURE 6.11**
Token

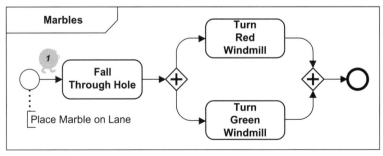

**FIGURE 6.12**
Place Marble

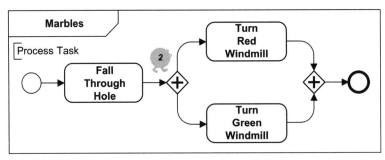

**FIGURE 6.13**
Process Task

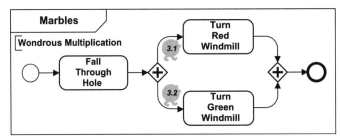

**FIGURE 6.14**
Split Sequence Flow

Each token now starts up its activity. Upon completion, each token goes via the sequence flow to the second parallel gateway where the flow is synchronized (Figure 6.15).

Only if a token has arrived at every inbound parallel branch are the tokens joined into one single token, and the flow is continued (Figure 6.16).

The token now enters an end event where it is destroyed (Figure 6.17). If no other token is active at this time, the entire flow is completed.

So a process is complete when the last active token reaches the end event.

Figure 6.18 shows the flip-book in one single diagram.

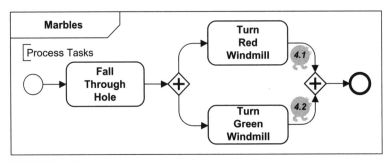

**FIGURE 6.15**
Process Tasks

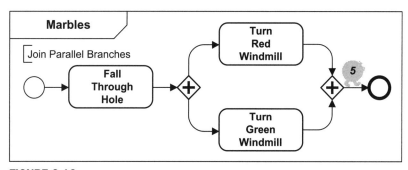

**FIGURE 6.16**
Join Parallel Branches

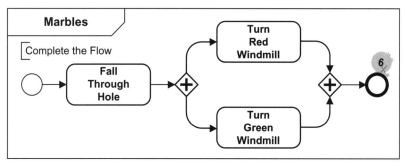

**FIGURE 6.17**
Complete the Flow

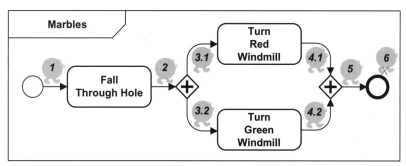

**FIGURE 6.18**
All Marbles at a Glance

# SEQUENCE FLOW

In a process, a token passes from flow object to flow object along the sequence flow.

## DEFINITION

A sequence flow connects flow objects and is used to show the oder that activities will be perfomed in a process.

| Sequence Flow | Conditional Sequence Flow | Default Sequence Flow |
|---|---|---|
|  | | |

**FIGURE 6.19**
Sequence Flow Notation

Sequence flow is used only to map flow sequences and not to describe the message exchange between pools (see Figure 6.19). Sequence flows beyond pool boundaries, between pools, lanes,[8] data objects, and comments are not possible.

Remember: A start event cannot have an incoming sequence flow. An end event cannot have an outgoing sequence flow.

> **DEFINITION**
>
> A conditional sequence flow is a sequence flow that comes directly from an activity and has a condition.

If the condition is true, the conditional sequence flow receives a token after the activity has been completed. Similar to the gateway symbol, the conditional sequence flow includes a little diamond. It must never come directly from a gateway or an event. If an activity has several conditional sequence flows, every sequence flow whose condition is met receives a token. In contrast to the exclusive gateway, the conditions don't have to be mutually exclusive.

> **DEFINITION**
>
> A default sequence flow receives a token whenever no condition of the other outgoing sequence flows is met.

A default sequence flow is indicated with a slash (Figure 6.20). If no condition is true at a branch, the default sequence flow ensures that the token and thus the flow don't get stuck. A default sequence flow can originate at an exclusive gateway or an activity. Our recommendation: Cover the entire value range at a branch using the default sequence flow. This way, you avoid flows that get stuck.

If several sequence flows without condition leave an activity, the flow is split in parallel (left diagram in Figure 6.21). Each outgoing flow receives a token.

Watch out! If multiple sequence flows run in an activity, this involves OR semantics. For each incoming token, the activity is executed once (right diagram in Figure 6.21).

---

[8]Sequence flow can only connect flow elements in different lanes within a pool. Two lanes cannot be connected directly.

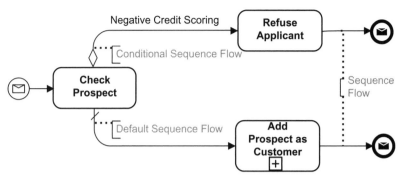

**FIGURE 6.20**
Example with Sequence Flows

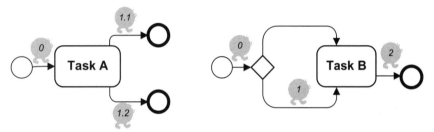

**FIGURE 6.21**
Parallel and Alternative Sequence Flow

# ACTIVITIES

Business processes consist of work steps that require resources and are executed by organization units or IT systems, for example. In BPMN, work steps are modeled using activities.

## Activity: Task, Subprocess, Processes

> **DEFINITION**
>
> An activity is a generic term for work that a company or organization performs via business processes.

An activity can either be a task, a subprocess, or a process (see Figure 6.22).

> **DEFINITION**
>
> A task is an atomic activity that is included within a process. A task is used when the work in the process is not broken down to a finer level of process model detail.

Task

To ensure that you don't have to cover entire walls of your office with complex processes, BPMN provides you with a construct for hierarchization: the subprocess.

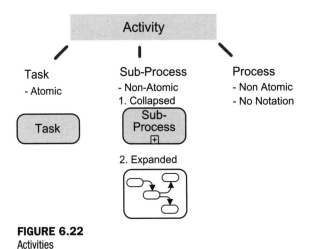

**FIGURE 6.22**
Activities

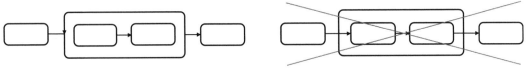

> **DEFINITION**
>
> A sub-process is a compound activity in that it has detail that is defined as a flow of other activities.

There are two notation forms for subprocesses: expanded and collapsed. The interior of an expanded subprocess diagrams its detailed flow. Incoming and outgoing sequence flow must never be connected with the internal elements, but only with the boundary of the subprocess (see Figure 6.23).

A collapsed subprocess refers to a separate diagram that contains the detailed flow. The collapsed subprocess bears a "+" sign at the lower activity boundary as a marker, which you can see in Figure 6.24.

Besides tasks and subprocesses, activities can also include processes.

> **DEFINITION**
>
> A process is a sequence of activities that are supported by one or more participants.

Processes present flows at different levels of abstraction. For example, a process can be used to map enterprisewide or job-related procedures. A sequence of activities within a pool involves a process, for example. A BPD may include several

**FIGURE 6.23**
Sequence Flows and Expanded Subprocesses

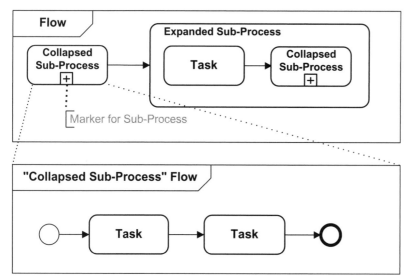

**FIGURE 6.24**
Collapsed and Expanded Subprocess

processes because it can consist of several pools. BPMN has no separate graphical symbol for a process.

## Activity Types

If you want to map an activity with a special behavior, BPMN provides you with predefined activity types. An activity that is repeated several times is an example for this. This activity is called standard loop activity and can be indicated with a graphical symbol.

Figure 6.25 provides an overview of all activity types.

You should know the various activity types and their symbols for the examination. For example, you should know the definition of a compensation. How these concepts are used for modeling is not tested in detail until you reach the intermediate and advanced examination levels.

*DEFINITIONS AND DESCRIPTIONS*

There are two types of loops: the standard loop task and the multiple instance loop.

> **DEFINITION**
>
> The activity of a standard loop task or a standard loop subprocess is repeated until the loop condition is met.

Figure 6.26 includes an example for both loop types: Figure 6.4 already described a flow in which SpeedyCar creates an invoice for a customer.

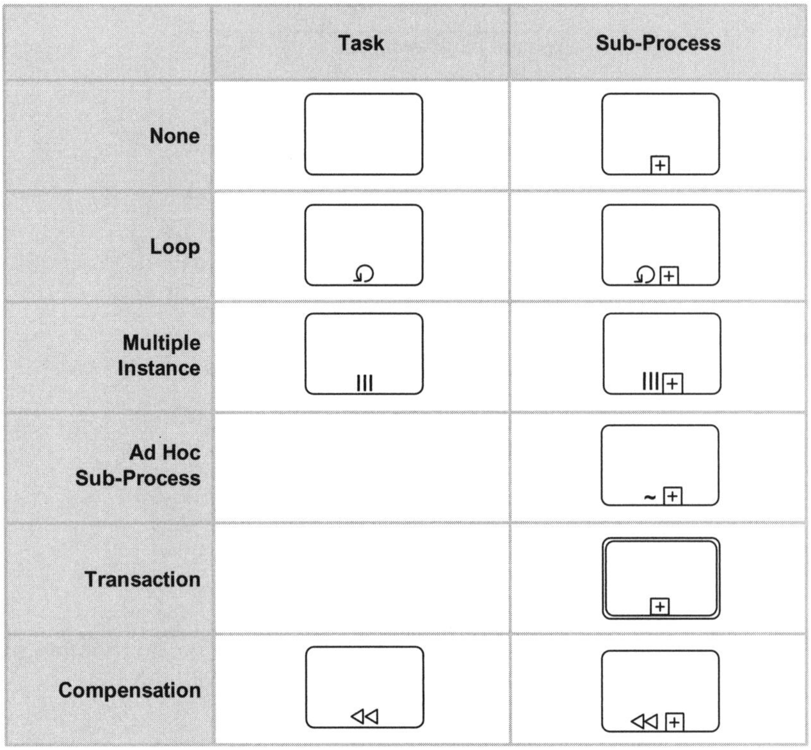

|  | Task | Sub-Process |
|---|---|---|
| **None** | | |
| **Loop** | | |
| **Multiple Instance** | | |
| **Ad Hoc Sub-Process** | | |
| **Transaction** | | |
| **Compensation** | | |

**FIGURE 6.25**
Notation Activity Types

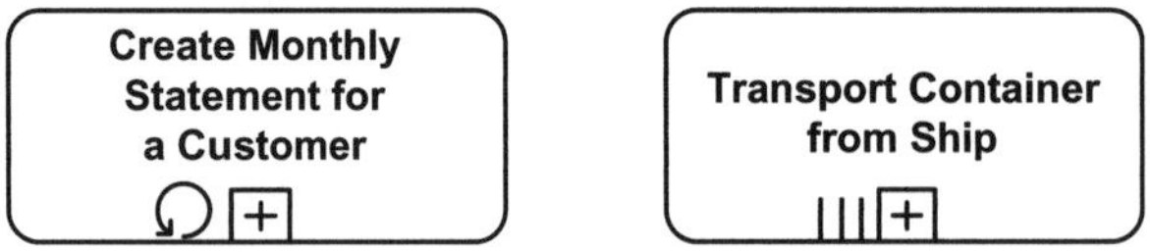

**FIGURE 6.26**
Loop and Multiple Instance

Using the loop, you can enhance this invoice flow in which monthly statements are created for all customers.

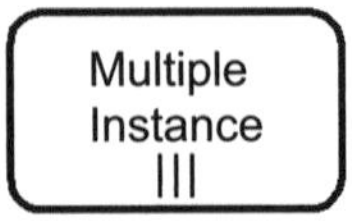

**DEFINITION**

The activity of a multiple instance is started multiple times in parallel or sequentially using different data.

If you've ever been to a harbor before, you've surely seen how a container ship is unloaded. Cranes unload several containers simultaneously from the ship onto a kind of fork-lift truck. The second example in Figure 6.26 maps exactly this case. Multiple instances (containers) are transported simultaneously from the ship.

Activities can have attributes, which are not visualized. The loop condition, for example, is an attribute of the loop activity.

> **DEFINITION**
>
> An ad hoc process is a group of activities that have no pre-definable sequence relationships.

Ad Hoc subprocess ~ ⊞

You can use the clean apartment ad hoc subprocess from Figure 6.27 to create a cleaning schedule for your partner. But you don't want to give too many restrictions. You therefore leave it up to your partner to define the cleaning sequence to himself or herself. He or she can start in the bathroom, then continue in the living room, and then finally clean the kitchen. Or he or she could first do the living room, then the bathroom, and then the kitchen, and so on. This is how you could model this plan.

Depending on the end condition, activities within an ad hoc subprocess can be executed multiple times. Accordingly, it would also be possible to clean the kitchen multiple times. Because an ad hoc subprocess is a random sequence, it doesn't contain any sequence flow.

> **DEFINITION**
>
> The transaction comprises multiple work steps that collectively form an indivisible whole.

Transaction

A bank transfer is an everyday example for a transaction (Figure 6.28). The amount is debited from your account and booked to a receiver account. The transaction combines the debiting and booking into an indivisible whole and succeeds or fails in its entirety. So it can never be the case that the amount is

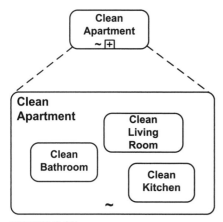

**FIGURE 6.27**
Ad Hoc Subprocess

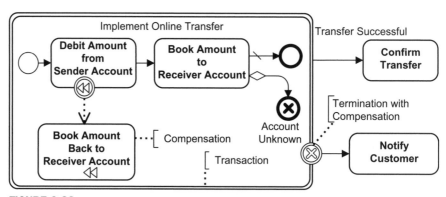

**FIGURE 6.28**
Transaction with Compensation

debited from your account without a booking taking place. But what happens if the transaction is terminated? How can you ensure in such a case that a consistent state is reached? At this point, compensation is used.

> **DEFINITION**
> Compensation is an explicit reverse action and describes the steps that must be reversed if a transaction is triggered to a failure.

The compensation's task is to establish a consistent state after a terminated transaction. If, in our transfer example, a termination occurs due an unknown receiver account, the token obtains an end state with the termination trigger.[9] As a result, the Book amount back to sender account compensation is called.

Consequently, the transaction failed as a whole, and the consistent state was restored. Then the Notify customer task is performed.

You can also combine activity types. For example, you can combine the compensation with the standard loop or multiple instance.

### Behavior Types of Tasks

In addition to the activity type, there are eight predefined task types that describe the behavior of a task. The BPMN specification in Version 1.2 has no specified symbols for task types.[10]

*NONE*

With this default value, the behavior of the task is not specified in more detail.

---

[9]The termination trigger is not relevant for the examination.
[10]BPMN 2.0 provides task types with predefined graphics.

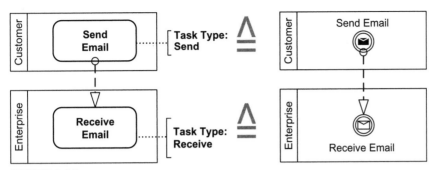

**FIGURE 6.29**
Behavior Type vs. Intermediate Event

## SEND TASK

The send task has one single job only: It sends messages to other external partic-ipants (pools). For this reason, the send task must not have any incoming mes-sage flows. The send task is an alternative notation form to the throw event with the message trigger.

## RECEIVE TASK

The receive task waits for messages from external participants (pools) and receives them. Once a message is received, the task is completed and the token leaves the task. A receive task must not have any outgoing message flows. The receive event with the message trigger is equivalent to the receive task. The modeling form you choose—task or event—depends on your modeling style and should ideally be specified in your company's established modeling principles (Figure 6.29).

## MANUAL TASK

Filing a letter is an example for a manual task. Manual tasks don't require any IT support and have neither incoming nor outgoing message flows.

## USER TASK

A user task is a semi-automated step, for example, entering a PIN number at an ATM. If incoming message flows exist, the task receives them when it is started. Outgoing message flows don't send their messages until the task is completed.

## SERVICE TASK

A service task is an automatable application such as providing a web service. Mes-sage flows are permitted.

## SCRIPT TASK

A script task is executed by a process engine and must not have incoming or out-going message flows. The modeler defines a script in a language that the engine can interpret.

*REFERENCE TASK*

A task of the reference type refers to a task in another BPD. This concept enables you to reuse tasks.

## Behavior Types of Subprocesses

There are two types of subprocesses: embedded and reusable.

*EMBEDDED OR NESTED SUBPROCESS*

The embedded subprocess is embedded in the parent process. Because the parent and child process work in the same global data space, the data doesn't have to be transferred from the parent process to the child process. Consequently, the embedded subprocess is independent of its environmental parent process and can therefore be reused in other processes where it works in its new parents' data spaces. An embedded subprocess doesn't have any pools and lanes. These are defined in the parent process. Moreover, the start event doesn't have any trigger.

*REUSABLE SUBPROCESS*

The reusable subprocess is depicted in a separate diagram. All data required is transferred explicitly to the subprocess. As a result, the subprocess is independent and can be reused in other processes. A reusable subprocess can contain several pools.

The default value for subprocesses is "embedded." Subprocess types are not identified using a notation element; you figure out what type a subprocess is by the way it is implemented.

## What Happens If an Activity Is Terminated?

If an activity completes without any errors, the token migrates along the sequence flow. But what happens if the activity cannot be completed successfully? For instance, what happens if the system crashes or the receiver account is unknown during the Implement online transfer activity in Figure 6.28?

There are three ways for the developer to model the response in BPMN if an activity was not completed successfully:

- The values of the activity before execution are written back. All changes that the activity implemented are therefore rejected.
- A reverse action, referred to as *compensation* (see compensation activity types), is called. The compensation defines which steps must be reversed.
- Nothing happens. Because the activity has not made any changes, no clean-up actions take place.

# GATEWAYS

You use a gateway to split and branch your process flow into alternative or parallel paths or to merge paths together.

> **DEFINITION**
>
> A gateway is used to control the divergence and convergence of sequence flow. Thus, it will determine branching, forking, merging, and joining of paths.

To model a gateway, you use a diamond symbol. A symbol within the diamond defines the gateway type and thus determines its behavior. A "+" sign describes a parallel gateway, for example. All five gateway types are included in the examination (see Figure 6.30).

## Exclusive Gateways

> **DEFINITION**
>
> An exclusive gateway restricts the sequence flow in such a way that exactly one alternative is selected from a set of alternatives at runtime.

Accordingly, the exclusive gateway corresponds to a typical either–or decision where exactly one alternative is selected. Or in other words, if multiple sequence flows lead from an exclusive gateway (decision), exactly one outgoing sequence flow receives the token. If an exclusive gateway merges a flow, every incoming token immediately goes through the gateway and continues the flow without delay (see Figure 6.31).

The conditions in an exclusive gateway don't have to be mutually exclusive. But what happens if two conditions in a gateway are true at the same time?

In this case, you as the modeler can specify a sequence in which the conditions are checked. As soon as the logic encounters a true condition, the token migrates along the corresponding sequence flow. Other true conditions are ignored.

Data-Based Exclusive
Gateway

Event-Based Exclusive
Gateway

Parallel Gateway

Inclusive Gateway

Complex Gateway

**FIGURE 6.30**
Gateway Notations

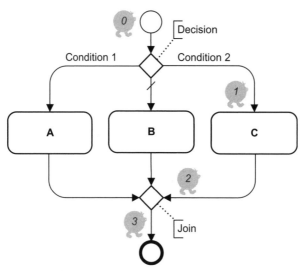

**FIGURE 6.31**
Data-Based Exclusive Gateway

You can imagine that this type of modeling sometimes leads to confusion. We recommend selecting the conditions for a data-based exclusive gateway in such a way that all conditions are mutually exclusive and the entire value range is covered.

There are two types of exclusive gateways, data-based and event-based.

*DATA-BASED EXCLUSIVE GATEWAYS*

**DEFINITION**

The data-based exclusive gateway decides, depending on the evaluation of a logical expression, how the token migrates.

The decision whether a condition is true or false is made at runtime based on the process data provided to the associated logical expression, hence the name *data-based exclusive gateway*. BPMN provides two equivalent symbols for modeling the data-based gateway (see Figure 6.30). Decide on a notation when you start modeling, and stay consistent.

*EVENT-BASED EXCLUSIVE GATEWAYS*

What happens if the process flow can be continued by different events? This case is shown in Figure 6.32. At the beginning of the process, a lecture is submitted. The process then waits until a reply is received by fax, e-mail, or telephone, or the commitment period expires. The event-based exclusive gateway modeled here continues the flow as soon as one of the events occurs.

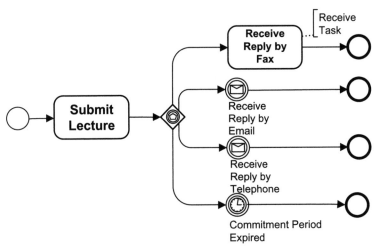

**FIGURE 6.32**
Event-Based Exclusive Gateway

**DEFINITION**

Depending on the incoming event, the event-based exclusive gateway decides which flow receives the token.

Event-based exclusive gateways are always directly followed by the incoming events or receive tasks. The token remains in the gateway until one of the modeled events arrives. As soon as that happens the associated event receives the token and continues the flow. In Figure 6.32, after the submit lecture task, the token waits in the exclusive gateway until it receives a reply by fax, e-mail, or telephone, or the commitment period expires.

*WORKFLOW PATTERN: EXCLUSIVE CHOICE AND MERGE*

To facilitate the modeling of recurring flow sequences, the BPMN specification refers to a number of workflow patterns.

The pattern for illustrating exclusive choice is based on the data-based exclusive gateway (see Figure 6.33).

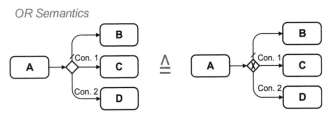

**FIGURE 6.33**
Workflow Pattern: Exclusive Choice

*OR Semantics*

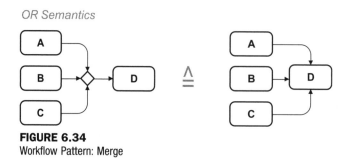

**FIGURE 6.34**
Workflow Pattern: Merge

The merge can also be modeled using the data-based exclusive gateway. The merge in an activity presents an equivalent variant (see Figure 6.34).

## Parallel Gateways

**DEFINITION**

A parallel gateway splits the sequence flow into two or more parallel flows and joins the parallel flows again. The synchronizing gateway waits until all incoming sequence flows have arrived. Only then is the flow continued.

When the sequence flow is split by a parallel gateway, each outgoing sequence flow receives a token. Conditions in the parallel sequence flows are not permitted. The parallel gateway at the end of the split process waits for all tokens for synchronization. In this case, the number of tokens corresponds to the number of incoming sequence flows. BPMN does not specify whether the activities A, B, and C shown in the example of Figure 6.35 are executed at the same time or not. It ensures, however, that the flow at the parallel gateway is not continued until all three activities have been completed and the tokens arrived.

*WORKFLOW PATTERN: SPLITTING AND SYNCHRONIZATION*

**Splitting**. The splitting workflow pattern can be modeled in two different ways: using the parallel gateway or an activity. If an activity has multiple outgoing sequence flows, every sequence flow receives a token when the activity completes. This notation is therefore equivalent to the parallel gateway. Both notation forms split the sequence flow into parallel flows (see Figure 6.36).

**Synchronization**. To synchronize a parallel flow, there is only one possible notation: the parallel gateway (see Figure 6.37).

The workflow pattern of the parallel box contains a subprocess without a start and end event. Let's simulate this flow. The subprocess starts, and every activity without incoming sequence flow receives a token (task B and task C in Figure 6.38). The subprocess is completed only when all tokens in a subprocess

0
1.1
1.2
1.3
A
B
C
2.1
2.2
2.3
3

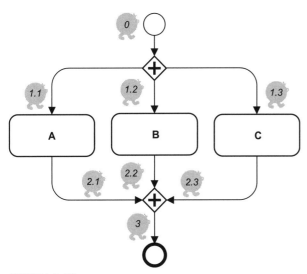

**FIGURE 6.35**
Parallel Gateway

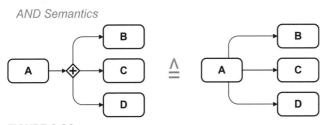

AND Semantics
A
B
C
D
≙
A
B
C
D

**FIGURE 6.36**
Workflow Pattern: Parallel Splitting

AND Semantics
A
B
C
D

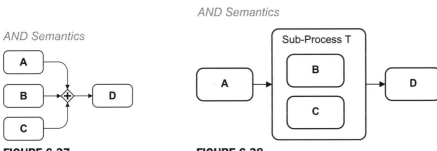

**FIGURE 6.37**
Workflow Pattern: Synchronization

AND Semantics
Sub-Process T
A
B
C
D

**FIGURE 6.38**
Workflow Pattern: Parallel Box

*AND Semantics*

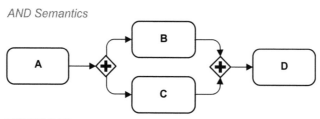

**FIGURE 6.39**
Workflow Pattern: Parallel Box with Gateways

have been destroyed. This is the case if all tasks without outgoing sequence flow were executed. As a result, the token leaves the parallel box after task B and task C have been completed.

The same flow can, as modeled in Figure 6.39, be illustrated using parallel gateways.

The example in Figure 6.40 shows, in contrast to the parallel box with gateways, a flow with two different gateway types. The type of gateway that splits a sequence flow can have another type of gateway that joins the flow again. However, such constructs are very prone to modeling errors, as this example shows. Because either condition A, B, or C is met, only one token arrives at the parallel gateway. This gateway, however, has three incoming sequence flows and waits for all three tokens. As a result, the flow is never completed.

## Inclusive Gateway

**DEFINITION**

In an inclusive gateway, sequence flow continues along one or more alternative pathways, depending on branch conditions.

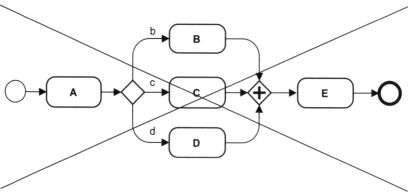

**FIGURE 6.40**
Deadlock

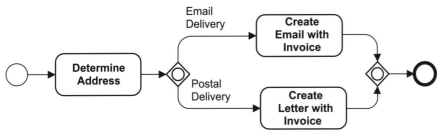

**FIGURE 6.41**
Inclusive Gateway

If multiple conditions are true at the same time in an inclusive gateway, multiple tokens run from the gateway. If only one condition is true, the inclusive gateway behaves just like an exclusive gateway. In this case, only one outgoing sequence flow receives a token.

The following flow variants are possible in the example shown in Figure 6.41. Depending on the condition, after Determine address, either one of the following activities is executed: Create e-mail with invoice or Create letter with invoice, or both Create e-mail with invoice and create letter with invoice.

An inclusive gateway that joins the sequence flow is a really smart little guy. It knows how many tokens are active and waits until all have been received. Only then does it continue the flow. On contrast, a data-based exclusive gateway would not wait here, but every token would directly pass the gateway and continue the flow.

*WORKFLOW PATTERN: INCLUSIVE DECISION OR MULTIPLE CHOICE*

The conditional sequence flow running from an activity and the inclusive gateway are alternative equivalent patterns for multiple choice (Figure 6.42). Multiple choice is also known as inclusive decision.

The inclusive gateway joins the multiple choice again (Figure 6.43).

## Complex Gateway

> **DEFINITION**
>
> In a complex gateway, sequence flow continues along one or more alternative pathways depending on a complex branch condition.

A complex branch condition could be the following: "Depending on the previous flow of the process, four of five sequence flows receive a token."

The complex gateway (see Figure 6.44) is used whenever it is not possible to map process logic onto one of the other gateways. Because the complex gateway hides the actual complexity and this frequently causes misunderstandings, you should use it only when absolutely necessary.

**FIGURE 6.42**
Workflow Pattern: Multiple Choice

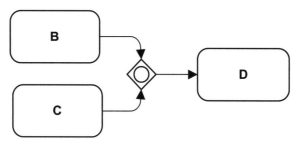

**FIGURE 6.43**
Workflow Pattern: Synchronizing Join

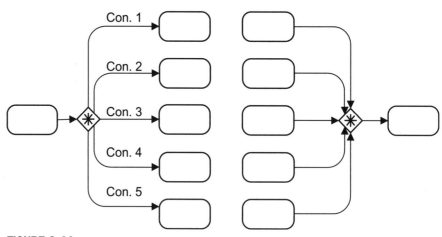

**FIGURE 6.44**
Complex Gateway

## EVENTS

Every year on December 31 at 12:00 midnight a special event occurs that initiates the new year. Events have a strong influence on flows in enterprises as well. If, for example, damage is reported to SpeedyCar, this triggers the process damage report process (see Figure 6.10).

| Start Event | Intermediate Event | End Event |
|:---:|:---:|:---:|
| ○ | ◎ | ⬤ |

**FIGURE 6.45**
Events Notation

---

**DEFINITION**

An event is something that happens during a business process and starts, ends, delays, or interrupts the flow.

---

There are three types of events: start, intermediate, and end (Figure 6.45).

An event is indicated with a circle; the start event has a single narrow edge, the intermediate a double edge, and the end event a single bold edge.

---

**DEFINITION**

A start event triggers a process and marks the beginning of the flow.

---

As soon as a process is called, the start event receives a token to start the flow. A diagram may have multiple start events. In this case, each start event receives a token when the process is called. Figure 6.46 provides you with a little example. If a complaint is received via e-mail, this complaint is processed. A complaint received via telephone also starts the process. If the complaint is received twice, once via e-mail and once via telephone, the process task is executed twice. (By the way—the letter in the start event signifies the message trigger; see the next section.)

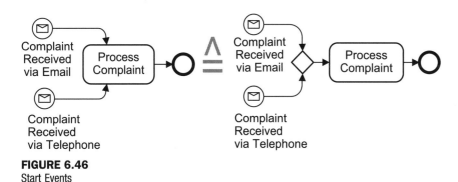

**FIGURE 6.46**
Start Events

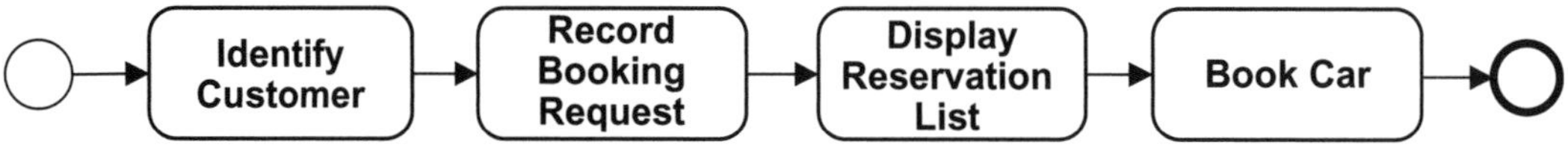

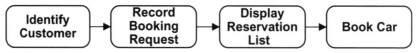

**FIGURE 6.47**
Book Car with Events

> **DEFINITION**
>
> An intermediate event is an event that occurs between the start and the end event and influences the flow.

> **DEFINITION**
>
> An end event ends the execution of the process and marks the process end.

An end event—just like the start event—can occur multiple times in a diagram. As soon as a token reaches an end event, it is destroyed. The entire process is completed only when all tokens have been destroyed. If an end event has multiple incoming sequence flows, this constitutes an OR operation. In other words, every incoming token proceeds along its sequence flow to the end event and is consumed there.

*FLOWS WITH START AND END EVENT*

Start and end events in a process are optional, but if you model start events, you also need to model end events and vice versa (Figure 6.47). According to the principle—all or nothing!

How does a process without a start event know which activity is actually started? In this case, all activities that don't have any incoming sequence flow receive a token when the process is initiated. In Figure 6.48, the Identify customer task

**FIGURE 6.48**
Book Car without Events

doesn't have an incoming sequence flow and therefore receives a token when the Book car process is called. Conversely, each activity without an outgoing sequence flow marks the end of the flow and destroys a token. After the Book car activity has been executed, it destroys its token. Because no further tokens are active in the process, this ends the entire process.

*THROW AND CATCH EVENTS*

Intermediate events can occur while the process is being executed. There are two types of intermediate events: throw and catch.

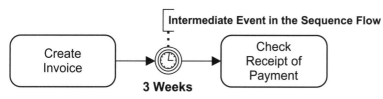

**FIGURE 6.49**
Intermediate Events in the Sequence Flow

In Figure 6.54, the throw event, Send application, occurs. When the token reaches the throw event, it is generated and the flow is immediately continued. When the token reaches the catch event, Receive application, it behaves differently. Here, the token waits until the intermediate event is received. Only then is the flow continued. The symbol for throw events is complementary to the catch events (see Figure 6.53).

An intermediate event can be modeled at two positions: in the sequence flow or on the boundary of an activity.

### INTERMEDIATE EVENT IN THE SEQUENCE FLOW

If the intermediate event is in the sequence flow, the process generates the event at exactly this position or delays the flow until the described event occurs. An intermediate event in the sequence flow has only one incoming and one outgoing sequence flow.

After the create invoice task, the token waits until the time event arrives (i.e., three weeks). Only then does it migrate to the check receipt of payment task (see Figure 6.49).

### INTERMEDIATE EVENT ON THE BOUNDARY OF AN ACTIVITY

An intermediate event on the boundary of an activity functions like an eavesdropper and cancels the activity as soon as that event occurs. This construct is deployed for troubleshooting, among other things.

An intermediate event on the boundary of an activity has no incoming sequence flow and exactly one outgoing sequence flow.

For example, if the driver in Figure 6.50 exceeds the end of the booking period, the intermediate result receives a token and cancels the Use car during the booking period activity. Then the Inform user about end of booking task is performed.

In Figures 6.51 and 6.52 you can find two examples that seem to be very similar at first glance. But are they really identical?

Subprocess T in Figure 6.51 may execute for one hour until it is canceled. This is different in Figure 6.52; here, task C may execute for one hour before it is canceled. In case of a time-related cancellation, task E is executed in both diagrams, and D is no longer reached.

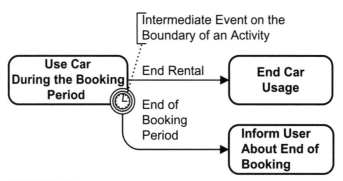

**FIGURE 6.50**
Intermediate Events on the Boundary of the Activity

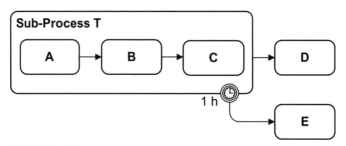

**FIGURE 6.51**
Intermediate Event on the Boundary of a Sub-Process

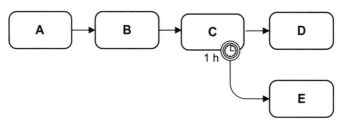

**FIGURE 6.52**
Intermediate Event on the Boundary of the Activity

| | Start Event Catch | Intermediate Catch | Event Throw | End Event Throw |
|---|:---:|:---:|:---:|:---:|
| None | ○ | ◎ | | ○ |
| Message | ✉ | ✉ | ✉ | ✉ |
| Timer | 🕐 | 🕐 | | |
| Terminate | | | | ● |

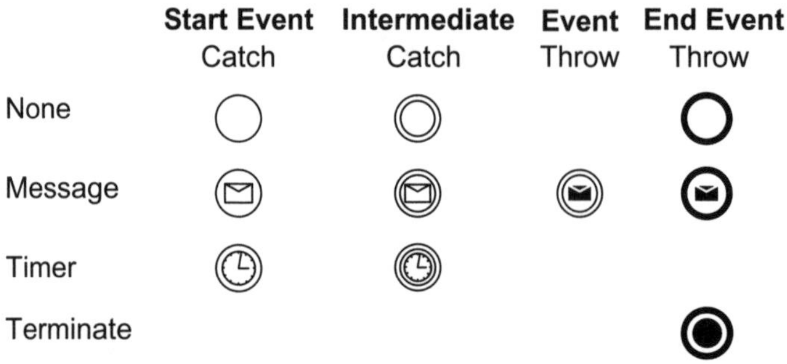

**FIGURE 6.53**
Events Relevant for the Examination

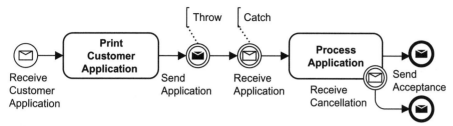

**FIGURE 6.54**
Add New Customer

## Triggers

The cause of an event—the trigger—can be marked with an event type. For the examination you should know the triggers message, timer, and terminate (Figure 6.53), which are discussed in detail in this section.

The symbol within the circle represents the type of trigger. An envelope stands for a message, a clock for a timer event, and a black circle for terminate. Watch out: The timer symbol has its own circle. In this case, the start event therefore consists of two circles and the intermediate event of three circles.

### TIMER

An event of the timer type starts the flow or continues it when the specified time is reached. A timer trigger can occur at a specific point in time (date, time) or a periodically recurring event (for instance, December 31, 12 A.M.).

### MESSAGE

Organizations communicate beyond pool boundaries using messages. In this context, senders and receivers are known. The message event can be used to express explicitly at which point in the flow a response is made to a message. A message can be, for example, a phone call, an e-mail, or a letter.

Figure 6.55 provides an overview of all permitted message events. You should know the various events, triggers, and their behavior for the examination. For example, if you have an end event with a message trigger, the process ends and a message is sent.

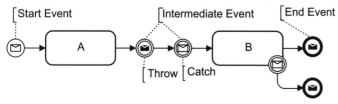

**FIGURE 6.55**
Events of the Message Type

Messages can only be used for communication between participants from different pools. They are not permitted for the communication between lanes within a pool.

*TERMINATE*

When a token enters an event of the terminate type, all activities are canceled immediately and the entire process ends. This is the main switch-off process, so to speak. The incoming token and all other active tokens in the process are switched off immediately.

An end event without a specified event type corresponds to a light switch; that is, only the incoming token is switched off. If other tokens are still active in the process, they remain unaffected and can continue their flow.

A subprocess cannot terminate its superordinate processes (parent processes) through a terminate event.

Besides the event types timer, message, and terminate, BPMN distinguishes a whole series of other event types that are particularly significant in the modeling of automated processes. Not every event type exists as a start, intermediate, or end event. For example, the timer event can be used only as a start or intermediate event, but not as an end event.

## SWIMLANES AND MESSAGE FLOWS

Frequently, different roles, such as customer, organization units, or an IT system participate in the handling of a business flow. Swimlanes structure a process according to organizational aspects.

> **DEFINITION**
>
> A Swimlane is a graphical container for partitioning a set of activities from other activities.

There are two types of swimlanes: pools and lanes (Figure 6.56), as described in the next sections.

### Pool

> **DEFINITION**
>
> A pool represents a participant in a process and acts as the container for the sequence flow between activities.

Customers, vendors, or your own enterprise are examples for pools. A pool comprises a set of flow objects (activities, gateways, and events) and separates them from other pools.

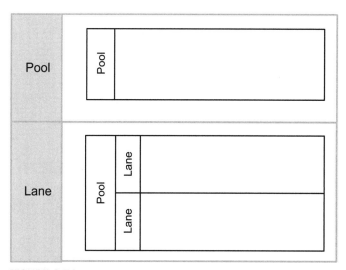

**FIGURE 6.56**
Notation Pools and Lanes

Pools can be aligned vertically or horizontally (see Figure 6.57).

Every process is always located in a pool. The pool representing the enterprise is optional in an enterprise-internal process. As a result, a maximum of one pool can be omitted in each diagram. In a collaborating business process, the participants are modeled using pools (see Chapter 3).

If the flow within a pool is not relevant, the pool can be displayed as a "black box." This way, the actual flow within the pool is hidden, like in the example of customer and SpeedyCar shown in Figure 6.59.

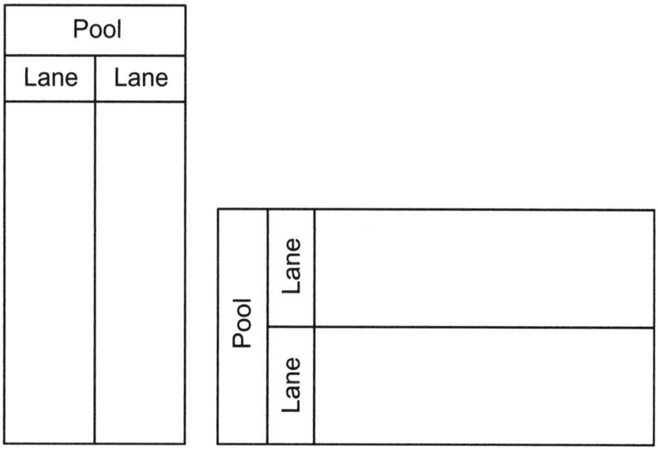

**FIGURE 6.57**
Horizontal and Vertical Pools

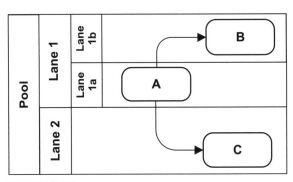

**FIGURE 6.58**
Sequence Flow Across Lane Boundaries

## Lane

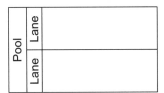

> **DEFINITION**
> A lane is a sub-partition within a pool. Lanes are used to organize and categorize activities.

Internal organization units or roles correspond to lanes, for example. A pool can contain multiple lanes, but each lane must always be completely within a single pool. Lanes can be further subdivided into more lanes too. All activities are always completely within a pool or within a lane.

## Message Flows

A participant, such as an enterprise, is responsible for its internal flows; that is, the sequence flow within its pool. Participants use messages to communicate with one another. How a pool responds to an incoming message is not the responsibility of the enterprise that sent the message. Or, in other words, pools are responsible for their sequence flow, but not for another participant's response to its message flow. For this reason, a distinction is made between sequence flow and message flow. Tokens always run along the sequence flow and symbolize the flow. As shown in Figure 6.58, sequence flow also links flow objects that are located in different lanes. In contrast to communication between pools, communication between lanes using message flow is not allowed.

> **DEFINITION**
> Message flow symbolizes the information that is exchanged between participants (pools).

A message flow is used to show the flow of messages between two participants (pools) that are prepared to send and receive them. Pools communicate only

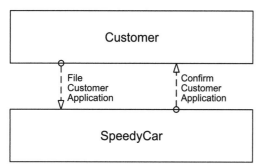

**FIGURE 6.59**
Message Flows Between Pools

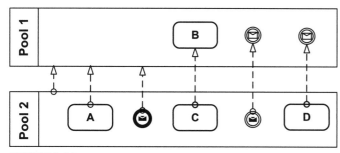

**FIGURE 6.60**
Example for Permitted Connections

via message flow (Figure 6.60). Communication partners must exchange their public interfaces to ensure a successful communication.

The following connection rules for message flows must be taken into account. Message flows are permitted

- Between two separate pools
- Between pool and flow object
- Between two flow objects

Figure 6.60 provides examples for all three connection rules. In Figure 6.61, you can begin to search for errors.

The following errors occurred:

- Error 1: Sequence flow between pools is not permitted.
- Error 2: The direction of the message flow is incorrect. It must lead from the throw to the catch event.
- Error 3: Flow objects must never be on the boundary of a pool or a lane.
- Error 4: Message flows between lanes are not permitted.
- Error 5: Flow objects must never be on the boundary of a pool or a lane.

Figure 6.67 provides an example with pools, lanes, and messages flows in the context of SpeedyCar.

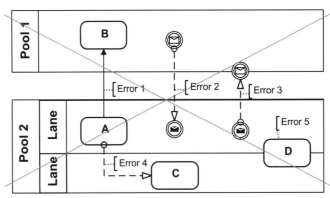

**FIGURE 6.61**
Erroneous Diagram

| Group | Text Annotation | Data Object |
|---|---|---|
| | Additional Information Can Be Mapped Using Text Annotations | Data Objects [State] |

**FIGURE 6.62**
Artifacts

# ARTIFACTS

To enrich a process or its elements with additional information, BPMN provides the concept of artifacts (Figure 6.62).

> **DEFINITION**
>
> An artifact is a graphical object that provides supporting information about the process or elements within the process. However, it does not directly affect the flow of the process. Artifacts include groups, text annotations, and data objects.

## Group

Let's take a look at the following application scenario: A sequence of activities that run across multiple pools is to be documented. Because subprocesses may only be within a pool, you require another mechanism here: the group (see Figure 6.63).

Groups are used to document related elements.

> **DEFINITION**
>
> The group object is a visual mechanism to group elements of a diagram informally.

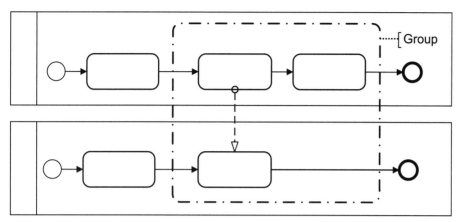

**FIGURE 6.63**
Group across Pool Boundaries

Because a group assumes the role of a comment, it has no influence on the flow. A group is neither a source nor a target for sequence and message flows.

## Text Annotation

You are probably familiar with the situation in which you properly modeled a rather tricky situation using BPMN and are not absolutely sure whether everyone interprets it correctly. A text annotation often works wonders here.

> **DEFINITION**
>
> Text annotations are a mechanism for a modeler to provide additional information for the reader of a BPMN diagram.

[ Text
annotation

The text annotation is represented with an open square bracket and can be appended to any model element using an association (see Figure 6.65). Like all artifacts, the text annotation has no impact on the sequence flow.

## Association

Information, such as text annotations and data objects, can be appended to the model elements to be documented using the association.

> **DEFINITION**
>
> An association is used to associate information and artifacts (text annotations and datat objects) with flow objects.

Associations can be directional or nondirectional and are modeled with a dotted line (Figure 6.64).

**FIGURE 6.64**
Notation Association

| Non-Directional Association | Directional Association | Bidirectional Association |
|---|---|---|
| ............... | ............> <............ | <............> |

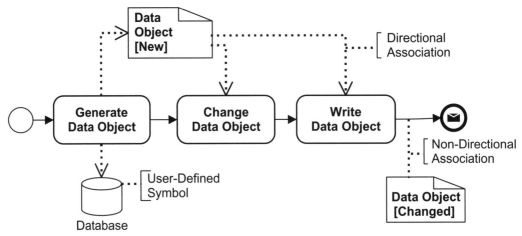

**FIGURE 6.65**
Data Objects with Associations

## Data Objects

Processes operate on business objects. Data objects are used if it is important which business object an activity creates, changes, or destroys.

> **DEFINITION**
>
> A data object is a business object that can be generated, required, changed, or destroyed by an activity. Moreover, a data object can have a specific state.

The note symbol is the symbol for the data object. The state is indicated in square brackets below the name of the data object and is optional (see Figure 6.65).

Besides the predefined note symbol, you can also define your own symbols for data objects, for instance, a cylinder for a database object.

An association connects a data object with a flow object (activity, gateway, or event), a message flow, or a sequence flow. As illustrated in Figure 6.66, directional associations between data objects and message or sequence flows are not permitted.

There are various options to connect data objects with other model elements.

The example in Figure 6.67 shows different variants with the same significance. The notations of the data objects "customer number" and "booking request" as well as "car list" and "booking" are comparable.

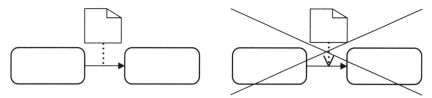

**FIGURE 6.66**
Associations Have No Direction in Sequence Flows

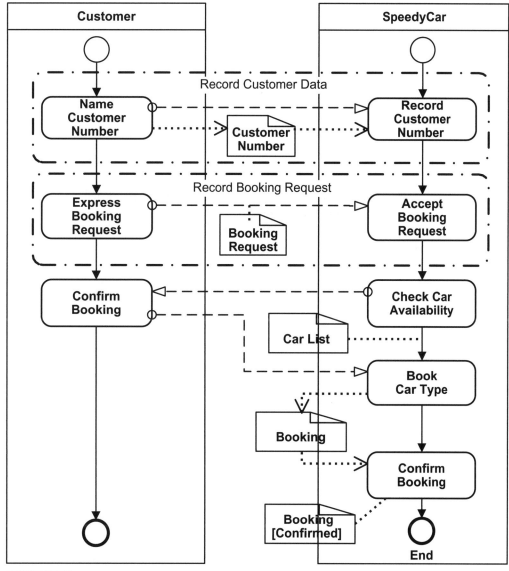

**FIGURE 6.67**
Book Car

## SAMPLE QUESTIONS

Here you can test your knowledge on the BPMN topic. Have fun! You can find the correct answers in Table A.5 in the appendix.

**1.** Which element cannot accept incoming message flow?
   **a)** pool
   **b)** activity
   **c)** start event
   **d)** end event

**2.** What are flow objects?
   **a)** gateways, activities, events
   **b)** any BPMN element
   **c)** message flow and sequence flow
   **d)** elements inside a pool or lane

**3.** Which types of connecting objects can connect elements of two different lanes in the same pool?
   **a)** sequence flow
   **b)** association
   **c)** message flow
   **d)** group

**4.** What statement is correct?
   **a)** The BPMN specification includes the specification of BPEL4WS.
   **b)** BPEL4WS is a machine executable process language.
   **c)** BPMN is a notation only for business people.
   **d)** BPMN 1.1 is a shortcut for Business Process Model and Notation.

**5.** Which notation represents a text annotation?
   **a)**
   **b)**
   **c)**
   **d)**

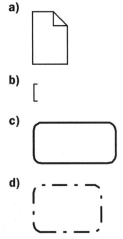

**6.** Which is an alternative representation to the given process?

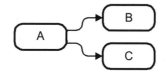

**a)**

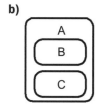

**b)**

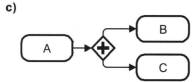

**c)**

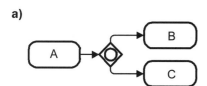

**d)**

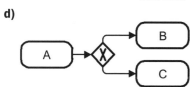

**7.** Which graphical element describes an association?

   **a)** o‑ ‑ ‑▷
   **b)** ⋯⋯⋯>
   **c)** ⋯⋯⋯▷
   **d)** ⟶

**8.** Which statement about pools and lanes is true?
   **a)** An empty pool is not allowed.
   **b)** A collaboration process is a process inside a pool.
   **c)** A pool represents a subprocess.
   **d)** An embedded subprocess cannot contain pools and lanes.

**9.** What is a generic term for work that company performs?
   **a)** event
   **b)** gateway
   **c)** activity
   **d)** group

**10.** Which statement about the diagram is NOT correct?

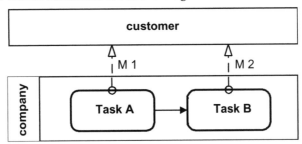

a) The diagram shows a collaboration between customer and company.
b) The pool "customer" is a black box.
c) Message "M1" is sent before message "M2."
d) Start and end events are missing. The diagram is not correct.

**11.** Which diagram describes the interrupt of task A if message M arrives and starts Task C next?

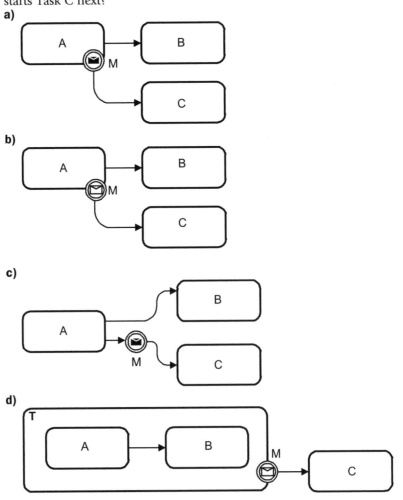

**12.** At first a customer wants to book a hotel. Then he wants to book a flight and a car or only a car or only a flight. Which diagram describes this situation?

**a)**

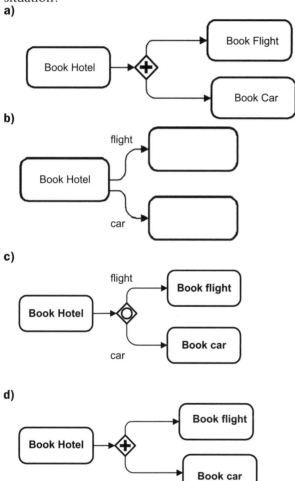

**b)**

**c)**

**d)**

# CHAPTER 7
# Frameworks

Example teaches better than precept.

**Samuel Smiles**

The last topic area of OCEB Fundamental comprises frameworks on processes, quality, management, and metrics, as well as regulations. It is not the certification's goal that you know the frameworks in detail, but that you are aware of their existence and that they can be considered or used in business process management. In your concrete project environment, there may be other frameworks that are of relevance for you.

Therefore, each framework is covered only generally. If you want to learn more about these topics beyond the certification, refer to their respective indicated references.

In addition to frameworks, this chapter also discusses basic terms from this area such as quality or regulation, principle, and guideline.

## DEFINITIONS[1]

Regulations, rules, guidelines, and other notations are terms that describe the directives. This section outlines their meaning. The subsequent sections then detail the concrete directives.

**Regulation:** A regulation is a directive published by a legislature, and compliance is mandatory. Punishments are possible if regulations are not complied with. An example of a regulation is the German Banking Law that, among other things, requires implementation of Basel II in Germany (see later).

**Self-regulatory rule:** Self-regulatory rules are contractual standards that organizations commit to on their own accord. For example, credit card companies such as Visa and MasterCard have committed themselves to the Payment Card Industry Security Standard.

---

[1]OCEB reference: Dorian et al., *Say What You Do* [9].

If these rules are not adhered to, this is not illegal, but it leads to contractually agreed punishments such as monetary payments or withdrawal of certifications.

**Principle:** A principle is a generally acknowledged rule. An example is OECD[2] Guidelines for the Security of Information Systems and Networks [15]. If you violate a principle, this doesn't result in punishments, but can have some unpleasant consequences because you have departed from a proven procedure.

**Guideline:** A guideline is a set of principles.

**Standard:** A standard comprises rules that were created and published by a standardization organization in accordance with a defined process. Nationally or internationally adopted standards are also referred to as norms.

Enterprises can also create internal standards for their own purposes; for example, to specify an enterprisewide guideline on business policy compliance.

**Control model:** A control model is similar to a standard, but one that focuses on the implementation of rules rather than the rules themselves. An example would be the Control Objectives for Information and related Technology (COBIT) (see later).

**Best practice:** A best practice is an accepted best approach to implement something based on experience. You don't have to pursue this approach and it is not always desirable because it is expensive, for example.

**Organizational control:** The organizational control is an activity that ensures that a directive, such as an organizational policy or a guideline, is adhered to.

**Organizational policy:** An organizational policy is a formal document that describes an organization's attitude toward a specific aspect. It impacts decisions and thus directs the organization into the desired direction. The set of organizational policies of an enterprise is also referred to as business policy. Compliance with its organizational policy is mandatory within the enterprise. If it is violated, this may lead to disciplinary action.

There's no concrete example of an organizational policy in the spectrum of topics of the OCEB Fundamental certification. The quality policy of oose is an example, albeit not relevant for the examination. It is available at the enterprise's web site (http://www.oose.de/ueber-uns/qualitaetspolitik.html).

**Organizational procedure:** An organizational procedure is a step-by-step instruction on how to implement a task. It directly supports organizational policies and must be handled as such in case of noncompliance.

**Safe harbor:** Safe harbors are prescribed shortcuts for the adherence to regulations. A standard would be an example of a safe harbor. If this standard is adhered to, the regulations addressed by it are adhered to as well. However, it is not true that the regulation is violated if the standard is not adhered to.

---

[2] Organisation for Economic Co-Operation and Development.

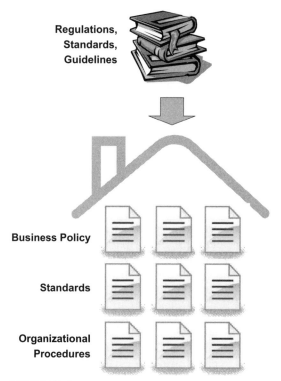

**FIGURE 7.1**
Corporate Governance

**Corporate governance:** Corporate governance is the set of processes and directives that lead, control, and manage the units of an enterprise (Figure 7.1). These derive from the enterprise's goals and environment and are significantly influenced by directives.

The term *corporate governance* also refers to the "enterprise code of conduct," that is, a sound behavioral code for enterprises. The OCEB certification, however, refers to the first definition.

# PROCESS FRAMEWORKS

Process frameworks are reference models that support the description, assessment, and optimization of business processes. They usually specify process hierarchies to classify processes. This way, you can classify your own processes in this hierarchy and compare, assess, and improve them based on specified metrics and best practices. It is also possible that processes are identified using the process categories. A process framework is a list of typical default processes.

Specific process frameworks addressed in the Fundamental certification include the APQC Process Classification Framework (PCF), the Supply Chain Operation Reference Model (SCOR), and the Value Reference Model (VRM).

## APQC Process Classification Framework[3]

American Productivity & Quality Center (APQC) is a nonprofit organization that offers assessments and best practices for business processes. Their Process Classification Framework (PCF) serves as the basis. It is a category model that categorizes a wide range of processes. Once you've identified the category that best matches your process, you can review its treatment to obtain the relevant assessments and best practices to compare, assess, and optimize your business process.

PCF is organized hierarchically. At the top level, you will find two types of processes: operating processes and management and support processes. The underlying level comprises five or seven additional process categories (Figure 7.2).

The process categories each include process groups, and the processes contained therein have a further depth of detail of the activities. In total, PCF describes more than 1,000 processes and activities. But don't worry, you don't need to know all of them for the certification. In the following, we describe the Manage Product and Service Portfolio process group from the Develop and Manage Products and Services process category including the Define product/service development requirements process and its activities:

**2.1** Manage product and service portfolio (10061)
**2.1.2** Define product/service development requirements (10064)
**2.1.2.1** Identify potential improvements to existing products and services (10068)
**2.1.2.2** Identify potential new products and services (10069)

Each process element has two numbers: A hierarchical number that describes the categorization in PCF (for instance, 2.1.2.1) and a serial number that uniquely identifies the process element in other APQC models also beyond PCF (for instance, 10068).

Concrete metrics and best practices are not covered by the OCEB Fundamental certification. Examples are available in the knowledge base on APQC's web site (http://www.apqc.org).

## Supply Chain Operations Reference Model (SCOR)[4]

The Supply Chain Council (SCC) is a nonprofit organization founded by Boston-based consulting firms. It develops and publishes the Supply Chain Operations Reference Model (SCOR).

---

[3]OCEB reference: *APQC Process Classification Framework*, Version 5.0.3 [5].
[4]OCEB reference: Supply Chain Council's Supply-Chain Operations Reference Model (SCOR), v9.0 [10].

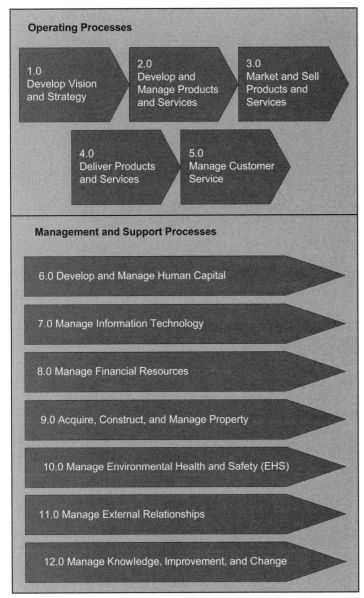

**FIGURE 7.2**
APQF Process Classification Framework

SCOR is a hierarchical reference model for supply chain processes. The model defines business processes, dependencies between processes, metrics, and best practices.

The top level comprises five management processes:

Plan → Source → Make → Deliver → Return

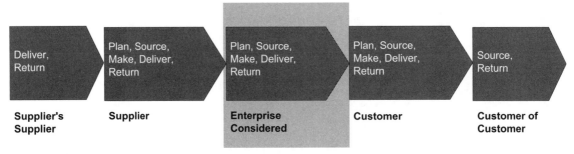

**FIGURE 7.3**
SCOR Process Chain

SCOR addresses a process chain wherein the five management processes only represent some parts of the chain. The process chain goes from the suppliers' suppliers, to the enterprise considered, to the customers' customers (Figure 7.3).

Along the process chain, SCOR considers product movements, the market, and the interaction with customers, going from the initial order to payment. SCOR explicitly excludes some areas including sales, marketing, research, development, as well as some elements of customer service after product delivery. Training, quality, information technology, and administration are addressed in parts only.

## Value Reference Model (VRM)[5]

The Value Reference Model (VRM) is developed and published by the nonprofit organization, Value Chain Group. It addresses the planning, governing, and execution of value chains to promote the effectiveness and optimization of processes. Their model supports enterprises in connecting business processes beyond functional unit boundaries.

For this purpose, the VRM describes reference processes on three process levels, each with the three core concepts of input and output, metrics, and best practices (Figure 7.4).

Strategic processes are at the top level. These have three categories: plan, govern, execute. At this process level, the decision is made as to how a value chain can be designed to gain a competitive advantage. An example would be a cost-optimized value chain in cooperation with partner enterprises.

Strategic level is followed by the tactical level. Processes at this level implement the strategic plan. This includes, for example, outsourcing of activities.

The lowest level comprises the operational processes. These are the most detailed processes in the VRM and describe the concrete steps, such as accept order or check order in the tactical process of procurement.

---

[5]OCEB reference: *Introduction to the Value Reference Model* (VRM) [19].

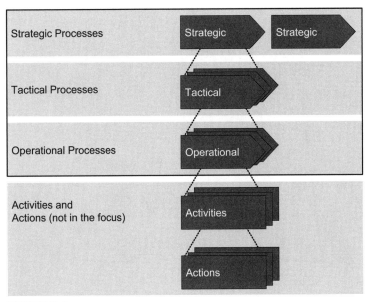

**FIGURE 7.4**
VRM Process Levels

Further levels of detail are addressed in the specification but will not be further discussed. Activities are refinements of the operational processes, and actions are atomic organizational procedures that cannot be refined further.

# QUALITY FRAMEWORKS

Quality frameworks support the improvement or management of the quality of a product or service. In addition to the basic aspects, the following section discusses the Business Process Maturity Model (BPMM), the Six Sigma quality methodology, the ISO-9000 standards, and the Toyota Production System (TPS).

## Basic Principles and Concepts

*Quality* is the central term in this section. But how is it defined? It is frequently associated with the criteria of reliability, usability, and performance. This certainly applies in most cases, but is not directly part of the definition of quality. Quality means to meet the customer's requirements. This condition can sometimes be met with products and services that don't have a high performance level or are unreliable.

Because the costs of error prevention are usually significantly lower than the costs of error correction, quality frameworks generally focus on improvement of processes that directly or indirectly produce products and services for the customer.

It is more effective to intensify process improvement than to increase the number of inspections that detect defects until they have already occurred. Depending on

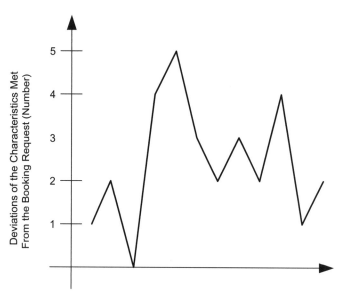

**FIGURE 7.5**
Example Run Chart

the industry, the focus of process improvement will be on different areas. Product developers, for example, should focus on the design of their products to prevent product errors from the outset.

To improve processes, you must first identify their weak points. This means that you must specify and measure indicators in order to reveal deficits. For this purpose, you require tools to present the measured indicator values appropriately.

To visualize deviations of measurement points from a specification along a time axis, you can use run charts. Figure 7.5 shows the deviations of the characteristics met from the original booking request at SpeedyCar, such as pick-up time, car type, car safety seat. They are used, for example, in the Six Sigma quality management methodology (see later). There, they are referred to as quality control charts.

You can graphically illustrate volatile data in heat maps. Variable value is identified with different colors. Heat maps are used frequently in meteorology.

There they are used to illustrate temperature distribution in maps—hence the name.

## Business Process Maturity Model (BPMM)[6]

You are probably familiar with Capability Maturity Model Integration (CMMI) [7]. It is a maturity model of processes for system and software development. The successful usage of CMMI at Nedbank Limited (South Africa)

---

[6]OCEB reference: *Business Process Maturity Model* (BPMM) [3].

suggested the idea of developing exactly the same model for business processes. This is how the Business Process Maturity Model (BPMM) emerged. With some intermediate stops along the way, the maturity model was handed over to OMG. That organization adopted it as a standard and maintains responsibility.

Watts Humphrey laid the groundwork for maturity models. In the late 1980s, he developed the process maturity framework at Software Engineering Institute (SEI). This formed the basis for the Capability Maturity Model (CMM) for software in the mid-1990s and CMMI in early 2000. Due to their common history, BPMM is similar to CMMI.

A total of five maturity levels exist (Table 7.1). Maturity levels 2 through 5 define process groups. These process groups must meet the goals of the corresponding maturity level in order to reach it. These are best practices that describe what needs to be done. However, they don't outline how this is achieved in practice. BPMM doesn't provide any methods.

A maturity level is not a universal solution that addresses all business processes of an enterprise. Maturity level 2, for example, includes requirements and configuration management, and maturity level 7 comprises further process areas.

Appraisal teams determine whether concrete business processes of an enterprise comply with a maturity level of BPMM. These teams consist of an external team leader and team members, some of them working for the enterprise appraised. The appraisers review process artifacts and interview process

| Table 7.1 | BPMM Maturity Level |
|---|---|
| 1 – Initial | The lowest level implies only that business processes exist. They are performed ad hoc, and their results are barely predictable. |
| 2 – Managed | Business processes can be repeated at the local level; that is, specific departments or teams (work units) are able to execute defined flows repeatedly. Similar tasks in different teams can be processed with completely different approaches. |
| 3 – Standardized | Standard processes derived from best practices are used. Directives specify how to adapt processes to specific needs. |
| 4 – Predictable | The performance of standard processes is recorded statistically to detect deviations. Process performance can be predicted or managed statistically based on intermediate states. |
| 5 – Innovative | Innovative improvement measures are actively taken to enable the enterprise to achieve its goals. |

managers as well as persons who execute the process. There are four different types of appraisals:

1. Starter appraisal: The appraisal only takes a few days to obtain an overview as to what extent the business processes of an enterprise comply with BPMM. Quantitative data is determined.
2. Progress appraisal: All process areas of a maturity level are examined in detail to advance development toward a maturity level or anticipate results of a confirmatory appraisal. Quantitative data is determined and compared with the review's results.
3. Supplier appraisal: This appraisal is identical to the progress appraisal, except that no employees of the enterprise examined are members of the appraisal team.
4. Confirmatory appraisal: All stipulated practices of a maturity level are checked in detail and examined with regard to the requested process goals of the maturity level. An organization can advertise the maturity level if it passes this appraisal successfully.

## Six Sigma[7]

Six Sigma is a comprehensive methodology for quality improvement. Only a few selected characteristics are covered at the Fundamental level of OCEB. Further elements are addressed in the Intermediate and Advanced levels of OCEB.

Six Sigma was developed by Motorola in the mid-1980s. In 1996, Six Sigma attracted great attention when Jack Welch successfully implemented it at General Electric.

The focus of Six Sigma is on the improvement of processes that result in products and services. For this purpose, Six Sigma provides comprehensive measures whose introduction and implementation require an appropriate infrastructure within the enterprise. Enterprise goals and strategies must typically be revised to implement Six Sigma, and they require new and adapted role descriptions.

The role names of Six Sigma are based on ranks used in Japanese martial arts. Figure 7.6 shows the hierarchy of Six Sigma roles. The Program Manager is responsible for the introduction and implementation of Six Sigma. Six Sigma Champions promote the Six Sigma program. They establish the new way of thinking and are responsible, for example, for assigning the Black Belt, Green Belt, and Yellow Belt roles. The Master Black Belt is an experienced Six Sigma expert who works as a coach and trainer of the Six Sigma project. The Black Belt roles are experienced Six Sigma users who usually manage Six Sigma projects. Green Belts are leaders in Six Sigma projects. Yellow Belts support Black and Green Belts. They can also implement small projects independently. The hierarchy of roles reflects the requested Six Sigma capabilities.

---

[7]OCEB reference: C. Gygi et al., *Six Sigma for Dummies* [13].

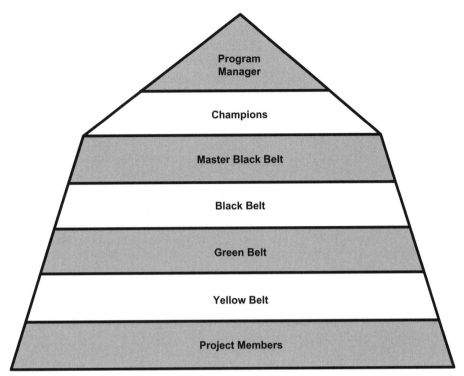

**FIGURE 7.6**
Six Sigma Roles

The core process of Six Sigma for process improvement comprises five steps. This process is named DMAIC after the initial letters of the process steps.

- Define the improvement goals: Before you can implement concrete improvement measures, you must first define the goals for improvement. You should only set off if you know where you want to go. Only then can you determine at the end whether you really reached your goal.
- Measure the current process: In the second step, you collect data on the actual processes. You measure various characteristics to be able to assess the current performance of the processes.
- Analyze the process: You know your improvement goal and the status quo of the actual processes. On this basis, you can analyze the process and reveal improvement potential.
- Improve the process: An effective improvement must be prepared well. Therefore, the actual process improvement is in the fourth position of the Six Sigma process. In this step, you implement the improvement measures.
- Control the changed process: Finally, you control the changed processes actively so that the measures have a long-term effect. This particularly includes the standardization of new measures so that they can be established permanently in the enterprise.

Six Sigma can be applied in four different focus areas:

- Thinking: Increase the efficiency of individual employees, among other things, by promoting their ability to assess things.
- Processing: Improve the processes with the involvement of all employees.
- Designing: Develop new processes. Only a few employees must be involved here.
- Managing: Executive managers manage the Six Sigma program.

In Six Sigma, a quality characteristic is referred to as CTX. CT stands for "critical to" and the X is in place of the characteristic. In concrete terms, this would be Critical To Cost (CTC),[8] Critical To Delivery (CTD), Critical To Process (CTP), and Critical To Safety (CTS). SpeedyCar, for example, deploys CTD of how long it takes from the application of admission to confirmation. The enterprise specifies a target for the CTD. Typically, this target is not always adhered to exactly in real life. The tolerance area is specified with upper and lower limits with reference to the CTD.

*PROCESS MANAGEMENT SUMMARY*

The CTXs are presented collectively in the process management summary. This is a tool of process monitoring to make all critical process output parameters that decide on the quality visible and therefore manageable.

Each quality control chart shows an individual quality characteristic along a time-dependent course (Figure 7.7). These are a variant of run charts (see earlier).

The Upper Control Limit (UCL) and the Lower Control Limit (LCL) form a corridor within which a quality characteristic meets the desired value or a normal deviation. Outside the limitations of UCL and LCL, the quality measured is considered as abnormal and requires intervention in the relevant process.

The unusual name Six Sigma relates to the deviation from the target value of a quality characteristic. Sigma (Greek letter $\sigma$) refers to the standard deviation from the mean value. Six Sigma therefore stands for six standard deviations. This is the required minimum clearance of the tolerance limit. If this condition is met, this means that a degree of perfection of almost 100% is in place.

The measurement unit for quality is DPMO (Defects per Million Opportunities). A process with 3.4 DPMO identifies the Six Sigma process quality. This means that only 3.4 defective results exist in one million opportunities.

Quality characteristics are output parameters of processes and directly depend on the input parameters. From the mathematical perspective, the following formula applies: $y = f(x) + \epsilon$, where y is the process output parameter (CTX), x the process input parameter, f() the process, and $\epsilon$ the uncertainty or deviation. The process management summary monitors the process output parameters, and the process control plan maps the process input parameters.

---

[8]CTC sometimes also stands for Critical to Customer.

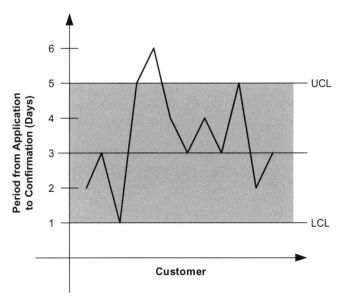

**FIGURE 7.7**
Example Quality Control Chart

## ISO 9000 et al.[9]

ISO 9000 standards specify a set of guidelines for quality improvement. The ISO 9000 series includes the standards ISO 9000, ISO 9001, ISO 9004, as well as ISO 19011.

ISO 9000 defines basic principles and terms. ISO 9001 specifies requirements for a quality management system. If an enterprise implements these requirements, and they are confirmed in an audit, it may use the known title ISO 9001 certified. However, the certification does not directly imply that the products or services of the certified enterprise are of high quality; only that the enterprise uses a quality management system that satisfies the requirements of ISO 9001. This should—but doesn't have to—lead to high-quality products. ISO 9004 is a guideline for improving a quality management system, and ISO 9011 is a guideline for auditing quality management systems.

## Toyota Production System (TPS)

Because the Japanese had to accomplish reconstruction on their own initiative after World War II, many effective procedures originate from this country or fell on fertile ground there.

---

[9]OCEB reference: Dorian J. Cougias et al., *Say What You Do: Building a Framework of IT Controls, Policies, Standards, and Procedures* [9].

The Toyota Production System (TPS) is a procedure for series production developed by Toyota. The goal of TPS is the productivity level of mass production in combination with the quality of shop production. TPS is better known as Just-in-Time production (JIT), which addresses a central strategy of TPS.

TPS avoids the storage of resources in the product development process. This is implemented, for example, with the zero stock concept, where no resources are kept in stock at all, but are purchased and delivered as needed.

## REGULATIONS AND GOVERNANCE FRAMEWORKS[10]

Regulations are statutory provisions. Business processes must adhere to them or new business processes must be implemented due to regulations. Regulations addressed by OCEB Fundamental refer to the financial industry only, but they are considered representative of further regulations from other industries. If you are responsible for your business processes, you must inform yourself about the relevant provisions and take them into account.

Governance frameworks specify how processes can be governed. Here, we only consider the governance framework Control Objectives for Information and related Technology (COBIT).

### Basel II

Basel II is a regulation for the banking and financials area created by the Basel Committee on Banking Supervision. Basel II consists of three pillars:

- Minimum capital requirements
- Supervisory review and evaluation process
- Advanced information disclosure; for instance, owner's equity structure

The European Union has required the implementation of Basel II in all EU countries since January 1, 2007. Implementation of Basel II in the United States is being planned.

### Sarbanes-Oxley Act (SOX)

The Sarbanes-Oxley Act (SOX) was enacted by the United States after the accounting scandals of the U.S. companies Enron and Worldcom. The goal of this federal law is to ensure the correctness and reliability of published financial data of enterprises whose stocks are dealt on the U.S. stock exchanges.

SOX is named after its sponsors Paul S. Sarbanes and Michael Oxley, who sponsored the bill in the U.S. Senate and House of Representatives, respectively.

---

[10]OCEB reference: Dorian J Cougias et al., *Say What You Do: Building a Framework of IT Controls, Policies, Standards, and Procedures* [9].

## Control Objectives for Information and Related Technology (COBIT)

Control Objectives for Information and Related Technology (COBIT) was developed by the Information Systems Audit and Control Association (ISACA) and the IT Governance Institute (ITGI) and was published for the first time in 1996. It comprises a range of best practices for IT management and control. COBIT links enterprisewide governance frameworks with IT-specific models such as ITIL.

COBIT is a top-down approach from the enterprise goals, to the derived IT goals, to their impact on IT architecture. The achievement of goals is measured recursively and thus results in a control loop.

COBIT defines a total of 34 IT processes and allocates them via 200 control objectives. Process and control objectives, activities, measurement parameters, and guidelines are described for each IT process.

ISACA also published instructions on how COBIT can be used in the environment of SOX and Basel II implementations.

# MANAGEMENT FRAMEWORKS

Management frameworks specify best practices, guidelines, and tools that support management in its work and monitoring tasks.

## Balanced Scorecard (BSC)[11]

Balanced Scorecard (BSC) is a management framework that was developed by Robert S. Kaplan and David P. Norton in 1992. It is used to compare measured key figures with the vision and strategies of the enterprise. *Balanced* refers to the balance between external and internal key figures. Management must take into account not only customers and shareholders, but also the internal processes and the further development of the enterprise.

The key figures of BSC are referred to as *Key Performance Indicators* (KPI). They are described in more detail in the next section. In summary, they form a key figure system—the scorecard—that is subdivided into four perspectives:

- Financial perspective: The shareholders' view focuses on the financial success.
- Customer perspective: The customers' perspective focuses on the vision of the enterprise.
- Internal business process perspective: The internal business process perspective focuses on the business processes that are necessary to meet shareholders' and customers' expectations.
- Learning and growth perspective: The learning and growth perspective focuses on the enterprise's ability to change and improve in order to reach the vision.

BSC is considered to be a strategic management system that supports critical management processes (Figure 7.8).

---

[11]OCEB reference: Robert S. Kaplan, David P. Norton, *The Balanced Scorecard* [24].

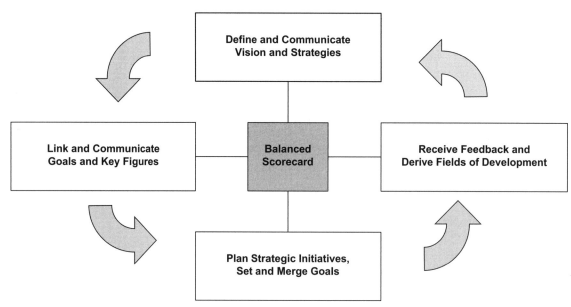

**FIGURE 7.8**
BSC as a Strategic Management System

## Key Performance Indicator (KPI)[12]

The Key Performance Indicator (KPI) is a business metric that measures the degree of fulfillment of a goal or a Critical Success Factor (CSF). The CSF is an organization-internal or organization-external property that is necessary to achieve a specific goal. A CSF can involve multiple KPIs.

Let's assume that your goal is to increase your average yield per customer from $10 to $15 by the end of the year. A CSF can be the marketing of a new product that hopefully has the result that customers spend more money on your enterprise. In this example, the KPI can directly address the degree of fulfillment of the goal. This would be the average yield per customer.

## SAMPLE QUESTIONS

Here you can test your knowledge on the frameworks topic. Have fun! You can find the correct answers in Table A.6 of the appendix.

**1.** Which BPMM level certifies predictable business processes?
   **a)** level 5
   **b)** level 2
   **c)** level 4
   **d)** level 3

---

[12]OCEB reference: Ed Walters, What are CSFs and KPIs? [35].

**2.** What are the top-level processes of SCOR?
   **a)** plan, source, make, deliver, return
   **b)** concept, analysis, design, implement, operate
   **c)** plan, produce, deliver, return
   **d)** manage, operate, supply

**3.** Which one is a process reference model for value chain processes?
   **a)** SCOR
   **b)** COBIT
   **c)** VRM
   **d)** VCG

**4.** What does quality mean?
   **a)** processes that perform without any errors
   **b)** processes that satisfy the needs of the customers
   **c)** processes that are optimized and predictable
   **d)** processes that amplify the goals of the company

**5.** What is Six Sigma?
   **a)** quality management method
   **b)** process reference model
   **c)** regulation
   **d)** management framework

**6.** The Just-in-Time production belongs to which method?
   **a)** Six Sigma
   **b)** TPS
   **c)** COBIT
   **d)** ISO 9000ff.

**7.** What is addressed by ISO 9004?
   **a)** quality concepts
   **b)** requirements for a quality management system
   **c)** guidelines to improve a quality management system
   **d)** quality maturity model for processes

**8.** Which domain is addressed by the Sarbanes-Oxley Act?
   **a)** health care
   **b)** automotive
   **c)** government
   **d)** finance

**9.** Which one is a collection of best practices for IT management and controlling?
   **a)** SCOR
   **b)** Six Sigma
   **c)** COBIT
   **d)** TPS

**10.** The process category Manage information technology is part of which process type in the APQC Process Classification Framework?
   **a)** Operating processes
   **b)** Business processes
   **c)** Management and Support processes
   **d)** Infrastructure processes

**11.** What was developed by Robert S. Kaplan and David P. Norton?
   **a)** Business Process Maturity Model
   **b)** Balanced Scorecards
   **c)** Business Process Reengineering
   **d)** Six Sigma

**12.** What describes a feature that is necessary to achieve a goal?
   **a)** Key Performance Indicator
   **b)** Business Process Metric
   **c)** Maturity Level
   **d)** Critical Success Factor

The important thing is to never stop asking questions.

**Albert Einstein**

## COVERAGE MAP OCEB FUNDAMENTAL

This section includes the official coverage map of the OCEB Fundamental certification [33]. There are seven topic fields in total. The percentages each indicate the weighting in the certification process.

### Business goals (8%): Chapter 2

- Business basics
- Strategies, planning, goal-setting
- Project management, marketing, staffing, finance

### Business process concepts and fundamentals (11%): Chapter 3

Fundamental aspects of business processes:

- Characteristics of processes
- Discovering business processes
- As-is process versus to-be process
- Levels of business process modeling
- Business processes, goals, and objectives

### Business process management concepts and fundamentals (10%): Chapter 4

- Function-centric versus process-centric organization
- Characteristic of process management
- Advancements in process management
- Stakeholders' roles and responsibilities
- Enabling tools of process management

### Business modeling (16%): Chapter 5

Business Modeling Fundamentals and elements of the Business Motivation Model (BMM):

- Vision, goals, objectives

- Means and end
- Mission, strategies, tactics
- Aspects of business modeling

## Business process modeling concepts (24%): Chapter 6

This section is based on Business Process Modeling Notation (BPMN):

- BPMN basics
- BPMN diagram elements
- Control flow and message flow
- Activities and decomposition
- Events and gateways
- Data objects, artifacts, and associations
- Grouping elements of a model
- Differences between sequential and parallel flows

## Business process modeling skills (16%): Chapter 6

This section is also based on BPMN. Instead of basic concepts, it examines the ability to understand these concepts. Most questions in this section ask something about a brief scenario presented either as a BPMN diagram or in a few sentences. BPMN elements and modeling topics covered include:

- Pools and lanes
- Activities and subprocesses
- Gateway logic: OR versus AND versus XOR
- Start and end events
- Timer

## Process quality, governance, and metrics frameworks (15%): Chapter 7

This section examines the awareness of industry reference models and quality, metrics, and governance frameworks: Covered frameworks include:

- APQC Process Classification Framework
- Supply Chain Operation Reference Model (SCOR)
- Value Chain Reference Model (VRM)
- Business Process Maturity Model (BPMM)
- Six Sigma
- Balanced Scorecard
- COBIT
- Basel II
- Sarbanes-Oxley Act (SOX)

# OCEB References

There's no single book that covers all topic fields.[1] The references are also part of the coverage map. They include concrete contents on the seven topic fields and are the source of the exam questions.

[32] S. Stralser, MBA in a Day; Chapter 1 (staffing), Chapter 8 (marketing, strategy, analysis of competitors), Chapter 11 (project management).

[16] T. Gorman, The Complete Idiot's Guide to MBA Basics; Chapters 1 and 2 (management: tasks and skills), Chapter 3 (enterprise structure), Chapter 8 (operative management), Chapter 9 (enterprise decisions), Chapter 13 (financial analyses), Chapter 23 (strategic planning).

[6] J.F. Chang, Business Process Management Systems; Chapter 1 (theory of process management), Chapter 2 (business process management).

[31] H. Smith, P. Fingar, Business Process Management: The Third Wave; Chapter 1 (development of the business process management discipline), Chapter 3 (enterprise processes), Appendix A (basic principles of action).

[26] M. Ould, Business Process Management: A Rigorous Approach; Chapter 1 (basic concepts of business processes).

[13] C. Gygi, et al., Six Sigma for Dummies; Chapter 1 (introduction to and definition of Six Sigma), Chapter 3 (essential Six Sigma concepts, DMAIC process), Chapter 10 (basic principles of process control).

[24] R.S. Kaplan, D.P. Norton, The Balanced Scorecard: Translating Strategy into Action; Chapter 1.

[9] D.J. Cougias, et al., Say What You Do: Building a Framework of IT Controls, Policies, Standards, and Procedures; Chapter 1, Chapter 2.

In addition to the books, the references also include articles. These are available for free on the Internet:

[28] J. Siegel, OCEB Definition of Business Process. http://www.omg.org/oceb/oceb-defbusinessprocess.htm.

[21] J. Hall, Overview of OMG Business Motivation Model: Core Concepts. http://www.omg.org/oceb/BMM Overview-Core Concepts - [081208].pdf.

[29] B. Silver, Three Levels of Process Modeling with BPMN. http://www.brsilver.com/wordpress/subscribers-only-2/three-levels-of-process-modeling-with-bpmn.

[25] D.J. Madison, Becoming a Process-Focused Organization. http://www.bpminstitute.org/articles/article/article/becoming-a-process-focused-organization.html.

[14] P. Fingar, Systems Thinking: The "Core" Core Competency for BPM. http://www.bptrends.com/publicationfiles/09-05%20ART%20Systems%20Thinking%20-%20Fingar.pdf.

---

[1]Except, of course, this preparatory book that you're holding in your hands right now.

[34] L. Verner, The Challenge of Process Discovery. http://www.businessprocesstrends.com/deliver file.cfm?-fileType=publication&fileName=05-04 WP Process Discovery - Verner1.pdf.

[35] Ed Walters, What Are CSFs and KPIs? http://www.12manage.com/methods rockart csfs kpis.html.

[5] APQC Process Classification Framework. http://www.apqc.org/portal/apqc/ksn/PCF CrossIndustry - Ver 5.0.0.pdf?paf gearid=contentgearhome&pafdm=full&pageselect=contentitem&docid=152203.

[10] Supply Chain Council's Supply-Chain Operations Reference model (SCOR). http://www .supply-chain.org/galleries/public-gallery/SCOR 9.0 Overview Booklet.pdf.

[19] Introduction to the Value Reference Model (VRM), Sections 1 and 2. http://www.value-chain .org/en/cms/?1960.

Of course, the references wouldn't be complete without the OMG specifications:

[3] Business Process Maturity Model (BPMM); Chapter 1 and Section 2.1.

[2] Business Motivation Model (BMM); Chapters 1, 7, and 8.

[4] Business Process Modeling Notation (BPMN); Chapter 1, Chapter 2, Sections 8.1 through 8.4, Section 8.6 without Section 8.6.1, Sections 9.3 through 9.7 (without attributes), Chapter 10 without Section 10.1.1.

# Glossary

## A

**Abstract business process**–The abstract business process describes the interaction between a private business process and one or more other participants.

**Abstract syntax**–The abstract syntax is a system of rules according to which permitted constructions are formed from the basic terminology of a language.

**Activity**–The activity is a step in a business process that is not further detailed.

**Activity [BPMN]**–The activity describes a job within a business process.

**Activity type [BPMN]**–The activity type describes a special behavior of an activity and can be identified using a custom symbol. Predefined activity types are loop task, multiple instance, ad hoc subprocess, transaction, compensation.

**Ad hoc subprocess [BPMN]**–The ad hoc subprocess comprises activities that are executed randomly, without a predefined sequence.

**American Productivity & Quality Center**–American Productivity & Quality Center (APQC) is a nonprofit organization that offers assessments and best practices for business processes. APQC is the publisher of Process Classification Framework.

**Appraisal team [BPMM]**–The appraisal team determines the conformity of a business process on the maturity level of the BPMM.

**APQC**–American Productivity & Quality Center.

**Artifact [BPMN]**–The artifact is a graphical element that contains additional process or element information, but doesn't influence the flow directly. Artifacts include groups, text annotations, and data objects.

**Assessment [BMM]**–The assessment assesses the neutral influencers on goals and means used.

**Association [BPMN]**–The association connects artifacts with other model elements.

## B

**Balanced Scorecard**–The Balanced Scorecard (BSC) is a management framework that compares key figures with the vision and strategies of an enterprise.

**BAM**–Business Activity Monitoring

**Basel II**–Basel II is a regulation for the banking and financial areas created by the Basel Committee on Banking Supervision.

**Best practice**–The best practice is the best approach to implement something based on experience.

**Black Belt**–Black Belt is a role in a Six Sigma project and a title for an experienced Six Sigma user who usually manages Six Sigma projects.

**BMM**–Business Motivation Model

BPD–Business Process Diagram

BPEL4WS–Business Process Execution Language for Web Services

BPM–Business Process Management

BPMI–Business Process Management Initiative

BPMM–Business Process Maturity Model

BPMN–Business Process Modeling Notation

BPR–Business Process Reengineering

**Break-even analysis**–The break-even analysis calculates the break-even point.

**Break-even point**–The break-even point describes the quantity of a product where the sales revenues cover the production costs (intersection of quantity-dependent cost line and the revenue line). If more products are sold, this results in profit. If fewer products are sold, this results in loss.

BSC–Balanced Scorecard

**Business Activity Monitoring**–Business Activity Monitoring (BAM) refers to the computer-aided collection, formatting, and presentation of business process data in real time.

**Business administration**–Business administration entails the governing and organizing of business activities.

**Business function**–The business function is a group of related tasks of an enterprise.

**Business Motivation Model**–The Business Motivation Model (BMM) is a standard of OMG and describes, on the one hand, the desired results of an enterprise with a superior vision and, on the other hand, the associated implementation strategies and tactics with their superior missions.

**Business policy**–The business policy is a set of organizational policies.

**Business process**–A business process is a business flow.

**Business Process Analysis (BPA)**–The Business Process Analysis (BPA) detects implicit process knowledge and provides it.

**Business Process Diagram**–The Business Process Diagram (BPD) is a diagram type of BPMN for presenting processes.

**Business Process Engine**–Business Process Engine is an application for executing processes. Here, the engine executes a defined sequence of activities.

**Business Process Execution Language for Web Services**–Business Process Execution Language for Web Services (BPEL4WS) is an XML-based language for describing business processes, whose individual activities are implemented by web services.

**Business Process Management (BPM)**–Business process management comprises coordinated tasks to record, improve, and integrate processes of the organization. In this context, the organization is considered as a system of linked processes.

**Business Process Management Initiative**–Business Process Management Initiative (BPMI) is a nonprofit organization founded in 2000 with the goal of developing standards in the business process area. In 2005, BPMI merged with OMG.

**Business Process Management Suite**–Business Process Management Suite (BPMS) is a collection of IT applications for supporting business process management.

**Business Process Maturity Model**–The Business Process Maturity Model (BPMM) is a five-level maturity model for business processes of OMG.

**Business Process Modeling Notation**–Business Process Modeling Notation (BPMN) is a graphical modeling language of OMG for describing business processes.

**Business Process Reengineering**–Business Process Reengineering (BPR) is a radical approach that propagates the new development of business processes instead of their adaptation. It was presented by Michael Hammer and James Champy in the 1990s.

**Business strategy**–The business strategy defines the direction into which an organization develops.

# C

**Capability Maturity Model**–Capability Maturity Model (CMM) is a maturity model for software development processes.

**Capability Maturity Model Integration**–Capability Maturity Model Integration (CMMI) replaced CMM in 2003 and addresses further disciplines such as systems engineering in addition to software development.

**CMM**–Capability Maturity Model

**CMMI**–Capability Maturity Model Integration

**COBIT**–Control Objectives for Information and related Technology

**Collaboration business process**–The collaboration business process describes the orchestration of the interaction, that is, the exchange like in abstract business processes and additionally the detailed process steps if required.

**Collapsed subprocess [BPMN]**–The collapsed subprocess refers to a separate diagram that contains the detailed flow of the subprocess.

**Compensation [BPMN]**–Compensation is an explicit reverse action and describes the steps that must be reversed if a transaction is terminated.

**Complex gateway [BPMN]**–In a complex gateway, the sequence flow runs along one or more borders depending on the complex branch condition.

**Concrete syntax**–The concrete syntax is the (textual or graphical) representation of an abstract syntax. Synonym: notation.

**Conditional sequence flow [BPMN]**–The conditional sequence flow is a sequence flow that comes directly from an activity and has a condition.

**Connecting object [BPMN]**–The connecting object is either a sequence flow, a message flow, or an association, and connects flow objects.

**Control objective**–The control objectives are areas that must be considered in a process to achieve the process goal.

**Control Objectives for Information and Related Technology**–Control Objectives for Information and Related Technology (COBIT) is a governance framework of ISACA that links enterprisewide governance frameworks with IT.

**Corporate governance**–The corporate governance is the set of all applicable rules, provisions, values, and principles for designing, governing, and monitoring the enterprise.

**Corporate Social Responsibility**–Corporate Social Responsibility (CSR) entails the corporate responsibility toward society, which goes beyond the statutory requirements.

**Critical path**–The critical path is the sequence of activities in a network plan with the highest cumulated duration. If an activity in the critical path is delayed, the finish date of the network plan is delayed as well.

**Critical Success Factor**–The Critical Success Factor (CSF) is a property that is necessary to achieve a specific goal.

**CRM**–Customer Relationship Management

**Crossover analysis**–The crossover analysis compares different scenarios with regard to fixed costs and variable costs.

**CSF**–Critical Success Factor

**CSR**–Corporate Social Responsibility

**CTX**–CTX is a quality characteristic in Six Sigma. CT stands for "critical to" and the X is in place of the characteristic.

**Current assets**–The current assets are the assets that are available at short notice.

**Current liability**–The current liabilities include all debts that must or will be cleared within one year.

**Customer Relationship Management**–Customer Relationship Management (CRM) refers to the systematic design of customer relationship processes.

**D**

**Data object [BPMN]**–A data object is a business object that can be generated, required, changed, or destroyed by an activity. Moreover, it can have a specific state.

**Data warehouse**–Data warehouse is a central, integrated data storage.

**Data-based exclusive gateway [BPMN]**–The data-based exclusive gateway decides, depending on the conditions in the sequence flow, how the token migrates.

**Decision tree**–The decision tree is a hierarchy-shaped visualization of decision rules and paths.

**Default sequence flow [BPMN]**–The default sequence flow receives the token whenever no condition of the other outgoing sequence flows is met.

**Defects per Million Opportunities**–The quality methodology of Six Sigma defines the quality measure, Defects per Million Opportunities DPMO, which indicates the number of possible errors in one million opportunities.

**Desired result [BMM]**–The desired result is a superordinate for goals and objectives.

**E**

**EDM**–Enterprise Decision Management

**End [BPMN]**–The end describes the vision of the enterprise and the goals and objectives derived thereof.

**End event [BPMN]**–The end event ends the execution of the process and marks the process end.

**Enterprise Decision Management–**Enterprise Decision Management (EDM) refers to the design of partly automated decision rules of an enterprise with reference to customer, employee, and supplier relationships.

**Enterprise Resource Planning–**Enterprise Resource Planning (ERP) is the targeted deployment of enterprise resources for an optimal flow of the business processes.

**Enterprise Service Bus–**Enterprise Service Bus (ESB) is an information technology for integrating a distributed application landscape into an enterprise.

**EPC–**Event-Driven Process Chain

**ERP–**Enterprise Resource Planning

**ESB–**Enterprise Service Bus

**Event [BPMN]–**An event is something that happens during a business process and starts, ends, delays, or interrupts the flow.

**Event-based exclusive gateway [BPMN]–**Depending on the incoming event, the event-based exclusive gateway decides which flow is continued.

**Event-Driven Process Chain–**The Event-Driven Process Chain (EPC) is a flow-chart from the ARIS tool and methodology.

**Exclusive gateway [BPMN]–**An exclusive gateway restricts the sequence flow in such a way that exactly one alternative is selected from a set of alternatives at runtime.

**Expanded subprocess [BPMN]–**The inside of the expanded subprocess includes detailed flow of the subprocess.

**F**

**Fixed costs–**The fixed costs are costs that are constant within a specific period of time and are independent of the production volume or quantity of sales.

**Flow object [BPMN]–**The flow object is an event, activity, or gateway.

**Framework–**The framework is a conceptual structure that supports the solution of complex problems.

**G**

**Gateway [BPMN]–**The gateway controls how the sequence flow spreads and merges within a process.

**Goal–**The goal elaborates the vision of an organization; that is, it describes the long-term goal that must be achieved to enhance the vision.

**Governance framework–**The governance framework specifies how processes can be governed.

**GRC–**Governance, Risk, and Compliance

**Green Belt–**Green Belt is a leader in a Six Sigma project.

**Group [BPMN]–**The group combines multiple elements that belong together logically.

**Guideline–**The guideline is a set of principles.

**H**

**Heat map–**The heat map shows volatile data in a two-dimensional graphic, in which the values are displayed in different colors.

## I

**Inclusive gateway [BPMN]**–In an inclusive gateway, the sequence flow runs along one or more borders depending on the branch conditions.

**Influencer [BMM]**–The influencer describes a condition that can result in changes to the end or means of an enterprise. An influencer can be internal (from within the enterprise) or external (from outside the enterprise boundaries).

**Information Systems Audit and Control Association**–The Information Systems Audit and Control Association (ISACA) is an international, noncommercial organization that supports the examination, monitoring, and security of information systems.

**Intermediate event [BPMN]**–The intermediate event occurs between the start event and the end event and influences the flow.

**ISACA**–Information Systems Audit and Control Association

**ISO 9000**–ISO 9000 standards specify a set of guidelines for quality improvement.

**ITGI**–IT Governance Institute

**IT Governance Institute**–The IT Governance Institute (ITGI) was founded by ISACA in 1998 to advance the development of international standards for the administration and control of enterprise-internal information systems.

**IT Infrastructure Library**–IT Infrastructure Library (ITIL) is a collection of best practices for the implementation of an IT service management.

**ITIL**–IT Infrastructure Library

## K

**Key Performance Indicator**–The Key Performance Indicator (KPI) is a business metric that measures the degree of fulfillment of a goal or a CSF.

**KPI**–Key Performance Indicator

## L

**Lane [BPMN]**–The lane subdivides and structures the activity within a pool.

**Loop task [BPMN]**–The loop task or loop subprocess describes executions that are repeated until the loop condition is met.

**Lower Control Limit (LCL) [Six Sigma]**–The lower control limit defines the lower limit of a quality characteristic that differentiates between normal and abnormal deviation.

## M

**Management**–The term *management* describes the process of letting things happen—by others.

**Management framework**–The management framework specifies best practices, guidelines, and tools that support the management in its management and monitoring tasks.

**Manager**–The manager is a person who organizes, plans, supports, defines, and assesses the work of others.

**Marketing–**Marketing is the market-oriented realization of enterprise goals and the alignment of the entire enterprise in the market.

**Master Black Belt–**Master Black Belt is an experienced Six Sigma expert who works as a coach and trainer of the Six Sigma project.

**Maturity model–**The maturity model is a model for assessing the quality of something.

**MDA–**Model-Driven Architecture

**Means [BMM]–**Means describe what the enterprise deploys to meet the enterprise object. This does not refer to employees or money, but to missions, strategies, and tactics.

**Message flow [BPMN]–**The message flow symbolizes the information that is exchanged between participants.

**Metric–**Metric refers to a measure system for the quantification of something.

**Mission [BMM]–**The mission describes what an enterprise does to achieve a vision.

**Model-Driven Architecture (MDA)–**The model-driven architecture refers to a software development approach that separates the subject-matter knowledge to be implemented from the necessary technology.

**Multiple instance [BPMN]–**The multiple instance represents multiple parallel or sequential execution with different data.

**N**

**Net income–**The net income is the remaining profit after tax and other charges.

**Network plan–**The network plan is a graphical, network-like presentation of sequence-dependent and sequence-independent activities (including duration, earliest and latest start and end date).

**Notation–**Concrete syntax.

**O**

**Object Management Group–**Object Management Group (OMG) is a consortium of international enterprises that creates and publishes standards in the area of modeling and interoperability.

**Objective–**The object quantifies goals. In other words, it makes them measurable.

**OCEB–**OMG Certified Expert in Business Process Management

**OMG–**Object Management Group

**OMG Certified Expert in Business Process Management–**The OMG Certified Expert in Business Process Management (OCEB) is a person who acquired a certification of the five-level OCEB certification program of OMG.

**Organization Structure Metamodel–**The Organization Structure Metamodel (OSM) is an OMG standard for describing organization structures.

**Organizational control–**The organizational control is an activity that ensures that a directive, such as an organizational policy or a guideline, is adhered to.

**Organizational policy–**The organizational policy is a formal document that describes the organization's attitude toward a specific aspect.

**OSM–**Organization Structure Metamodel

**Overhead costs**–Overhead costs are costs that can be allocated only indirectly to a cost unit (product, service).

**Owner's equity**–The owner's equity is part of the company assets that is left after deduction of debt capital (noncurrent and current liabilities).

**P**

**Parallel gateway [BPMN]**–A parallel gateway divides the sequence flow into two or more parallel flows and joins the parallel flows again. The synchronization waits until all incoming sequence flows have arrived. Only then is the flow continued.

**Participant**–The participant is an enterprise, a customer, or a business partner and is responsible for the execution of a process. In BPMN, participants are mapped using pools.

**PCF**–Process Classification Framework

**PEST analysis**–STEP analysis

**Pool [BPMN]**–The pool represents a participant and serves as a container for the sequence flow between activities. Pools can contain lanes.

**Porter's Five Forces**–Porter's Five Forces support an enterprise in selecting a suitable strategy to gain a competitive advantage.

**Principle**–The principle is a generally acknowledged rule.

**Private business process**–The private business process contains only process steps that are executed within the organization.

**Process Classification Framework**–Process Classification Framework (PCF) is a category model that categorizes a wide range of processes.

**Production Rules Representation**–Die Production Rules Representation (PRR) is a standard of OMG for the manufacturer-independent presentation of production rules.

**Program Manager [Six Sigma]**–The Program Manager is responsible for the introduction and implementation of Six Sigma.

**Project**–The project is an undertaking that is unique in its entirety with limited timeframes and budget to deliver clearly defined results.

**Project management**–Project management is the deployment of knowledge, skills, tools, and techniques in a project.

**Process [BPMN]**–The process is a sequence of activities that are supported by one or more participants. In BPMN, a process is a business process.

**Process control plan [Six Sigma]**–The process control plan presents the process input parameters relevant for quality. See also process management summary.

**Process discovery**–The process discovery is a process for discovering implicit process knowledge.

**Process management summary**–Process management summary is a Six Sigma tool of process monitoring to make all critical process output parameters that decide on the quality visible and therefore manageable.

**Process owner**–The process owner is responsible for the success of his or her process and has appropriate rights and duties.

**Process topology**–The process topology describes the structure of a process, that is, the flow steps and their interrelations.

**PRR**–Production Rules Representation

## Q

**Quality**–Quality means to meet the customer's requirements.

**Quality control chart**–The quality control chart shows an individual quality characteristic along a time-dependent course. It is a variant of the run charts.

**Quality framework**–The quality framework supports the improvement or management of a product's or service's quality.

**Quality Management System**–The Quality Management System (QMS) specifies the structures, roles, resources, and processes that are necessary to implement an active management of quality.

## R

**Regulation**–The regulation is a directive published by legislature and compliance is mandatory. Punishments are possible if they are not complied with.

**Return on Investment**–Return on Investment (ROI) is a financial key figure for assessing the profitability of an investment made. An investment is unprofitable if the net income made divided by owner's equity used is less than or equal to 1.0.

**ROI**–Return on Investment

**Role**–The role is the set of expectations toward a person.

**Run chart**–The run chart is a two-dimensional graphic that illustrates the deviations of values from a specification along a time axis.

## S

**SaaS**–Software as a Service

**Sarbanes-Oxley Act**–The Sarbanes-Oxley Act is a federal act that ensures the correctness and reliability of published financial data of enterprises whose stocks are dealt on the U.S. stock exchanges.

**SBVR**–Semantics Business Vocabulary and Rules

**Semantics**–Semantics describes and explains the meaning of a term of a language.

**Semantics Business Vocabulary and Rules**–Semantics Business Vocabulary and Rules (SBVR) are a standard of OMG for describing business objects and business rules.

**Sequence flow [BPMN]**–The sequence flow links the flow objects and therefore describes the flow sequence of activities in the process.

**Service Level Agreement**–The Service Level Agreement (SLA) is a contract between a customer and a service provider and defines the quality of interfaces.

**Service-Oriented Architecture**–The Service-Oriented Architecture (SOA) is an approach for the implementation of business processes in distributed systems, which is based on the individual business functions.

**Six Sigma**–Six Sigma is a methodology to improve processes in order to increase the quality of products and services.

**Six Sigma Champion**–The Six Sigma Champion is a driver of the Six Sigma program, establishes the new way of thinking, and is responsible, for example, for assigning the Black Belt, Green Belt, and Yellow Belt roles.

**SLA**–Service Level Agreement

**SOA**–Service-Oriented Architecture

**Software as a Service**–Software as a Service (SaaS) is a business model that provides software as a service.

**Stakeholder**–The stakeholder is a person or institution that has an interest in a project and potentially contributes requirements.

**Start event [BPMN]**–The start event triggers a process and marks the beginning of the flow.

**STEP analysis**–The STEP analysis provides references for considering the opportunities and threats of a market. Synonym: PEST analysis.

**Strategy [BMM]**–The strategy channels efforts toward the goals.

**Subject Matter Expert (SME)**–The subject matter expert is a person who has established professional expertise in a defined area.

**Subprocess [BPMN]**–The subprocess is a combination of detailed activities.

**Swimlane [BPMN]**–A swimlane is a graphical container that separates a set of activities from other activities. BPMN knows two types of swimlanes: pools and lanes.

**SWOT analysis**–The SWOT analysis considers the internal strengths and weaknesses of an organization and the external opportunities and risks in the market.

**T**

**Tactic [BMM]**–The tactic implements strategies.

**Task [BPMN]**–The task is an atomic activity within a process; that is, a task is not detailed as a graphic in the model.

**Terminate [BPMN]**–Terminate is the trigger of an end event that destroys all active tokens and therefore ends the entire process.

**Text annotation [BPMN]**–The text annotation is a textual description that can be connected with every diagram element via an association.

**Token [BPMN]**–A token is some sort of virtual marble, which is generated when a process is called and stands for a concrete flow along events, activities, gateways, and sequence flows.

**Total Quality Management**–Total Quality Management (TQM) is a methodology to improve the quality through active management of processes.

**Toyota Production System**–The Toyota Production System (TPS) is a procedure for series production developed by Toyota. The goal of TPS is the productivity of mass production in combination with the quality of shop production.

**TPS**–Toyota Production System

**TQM**–Total Quality Management

**Transaction [BPMN]**–The transaction comprises multiple work steps that collectively form an indivisible whole.

**Trigger [BPMN]**–The trigger describes the cause why an event occurs and can be identified using custom symbols. Examples are message, timer, and terminate.

**U**

**Upper Control Limit (UCL) [Six Sigma]**–The upper control limit defines the upper limit of a quality characteristic that differentiates between normal and abnormal deviation.

# V

**Value chain**–The value chain represents the activities of an enterprise that are performed to design, produce, market, deliver, and support its product.

**Value Chain Group**–Value Chain Group (VCG) is a nonprofit organization that develops and publishes the Value Reference Model.

**Value Reference Model**–The Value Reference Model (VRM) addresses the planning, management, and execution of value chains to promote the effectiveness and optimization of processes.

**Variable costs**–Variable costs are costs that vary if the production volume or quantity of sales changes.

**VCG**–Value Chain Group

**Vision [BMM]**–The vision is a meaningful, pictorial perception of the future of an enterprise that expresses an ultimate, rather unattainable, but desirable state.

**VRM**–Value Reference Model

# W

**WfMC**–Workflow Management Coalition

**Workflow Management Coalition**–Workflow Management Coalition (WfMC) is a coalition of manufacturers that develop and publish the workflow reference model und further related standards.

**Workflow pattern**–The workflow pattern is a solution guideline for describing a defined workflow sequence.

**Working capital**–The working capital is part of the current assets that is available for investments (after deduction of all debts that must be paid within one year).

# Y

**Yellow Belt**–Yellow Belt is a role in a Six Sigma project that supports the Green Belts and Black Belts and can manage small Six Sigma projects.

| Table A.1 | Solutions Chapter 2: Busi |  | |
|-----------|---------|---|---|
| 1 | b | 6 | |
| 2 | c | 7 | |
| 3 | b | 8 | |
| 4 | a | 9 | |
| 5 | b | | |

| Table A.2 | Solutions Chapter 3: Business Processes | | |
|-----------|---------|---|---|
| 1 | a | 5 | b |
| 2 | c | 6 | c |
| 3 | b | 7 | b |
| 4 | c | 8 | d |

| Table A.3 | Solutions Chapter 4: Business Process Management | | |
|-----------|---------|---|---|
| 1 | d | 4 | c |
| 2 | c | 5 | b |
| 3 | a | 6 | d |

| Table A.4 | Solutions Chapter 5: Business Modeling | | |
|-----------|---------|----|---|
| 1 | c | 7 | a |
| 2 | d | 8 | b |
| 3 | b | 9 | c |
| 4 | a | 10 | b |
| 5 | a | 11 | a |
| 6 | c | | |

| A.5 | Solutions Chapter 6: Business Process Modeling | | | | |
|---|---|---|---|---|---|
| | d | | 7 | | b |
| | a | | 8 | | d |
| | a | | 9 | | c |
| | b | | 10 | | d |
| 5 | b | | 11 | | b |
| 6 | c | | 12 | | c |

| Table A.6 | Solutions Chapter 7: Frameworks | | | | |
|---|---|---|---|---|---|
| 1 | c | | 7 | | c |
| 2 | a | | 8 | | d |
| 3 | c | | 9 | | c |
| 4 | b | | 10 | | c |
| 5 | a | | 11 | | b |
| 6 | b | | 12 | | d |

[1] M.J. Benner, M.L. Tushman, Exploitation, Exploration, and Process Management: The Productivity Dilemma Revisited, Acad. Manage. Rev. 28 (2003) 238–256.

[2] Business Motivation Model (BMM) Specification, http://www.omg.org/cgi-bin/doc?dtc/07-08-03, 2007.

[3] Business Process Maturity Model (BPMM), http://www.omg.org/cgi-bin/doc?formal/08-06-01.pdf, 2008.

[4] Business Process Modeling Notation (BPMN), http://www.omg.org/spec/BPMN/1.1/, 2008.

[5] American Productivity & Quality Center, APQC Process Classification Framework, http://www.apqc.org/portal/apqc/ksn/PCFCrossIndustry-Ver5.0.0.pdf?pafgear-id=contentgearhome&pafdm=full&-pageselect=contentitem&docid=152203, Version 5.0.3.

[6] J.F. Chang, Business Process Management Systems, Auerbach, 2006.

[7] CMMI—Capability Maturity Model Integration, http://www.sei.cmu.edu/cmmi/index.cfm, July 2011.

[8] Workflow Management Coalition, Terminology & Glossary, WFMC-TC-1011 (1999).

[9] D.J. Cougias, et al., Say What You Do: Building a Framework of IT Controls, Policies, Standards, and Procedures, Shaser-Vartan, 2007.

[10] Supply-Chain Council, Supply Chain Council's Supply-Chain Operations Reference model (SCOR), http://supply-chain.org/f/SCOR-Overview-Web.pdf, Version 10, 2010.

[11] T.H. Davenport, J.E. Short, The New Industrial Engineering: Information Technology and Business Process Redesign. Sloan Manage. Rev., Summer (1990) 11–27.

[12] W.E. Deming, Report Card on TQM, Manage. Rev. January (1994) 22–25.

[13] C. Gygi, et al., Six Sigma for Dummies, John Wiley & Sons, Inc., 2005.

[14] P. Fingar, Systems Thinking: The "Core" Core Competency for BPM, BP Trends, http://www.bptrends.com/publicationfiles/09-05%20ART%20Systems%20Thinking%20-%20Fingar.pdf, September 2005.

[15] Organisation for Economic Co-operation and Development, Guidelines for the Security of Information Systems and Networks, http://www.oecd.org/dataoecd/16/22/15582260.pdf, 2002.

[16] T. Gorman, The Complete Idiot's Guide to MBA Basics, second ed., Alpha, 2003.

[17] Object Management Group, Press release on the start of the OCEB certification program, http://www.omg.org/news/releases/pr2008/03-27-07.htm, 2008.

[18] Object Management Group, OMG Certified Expert in BPM, http://www.omg.org/oceb, 2009.

[19] Value Chain Group, Introduction to the Value Reference Model (VRM), http://www.value-chain.org/en/cms/?1960, 2009.

[20] J.R. Hackmann, R. Wageman, Total Quality Management: Empirical, Conceptual, and Practical Issues, Adm. Sci. Q. 40 (1995) 309–342.

[21] J. Hall, Overview of OMG Business Motivation Model: Core Concepts, http://www.omg.org/oceb/BMM_Overview-Core_Concepts_[081208].pdf, 2008.

[22] M. Hammer, Reengineering work: Don't automate, obliterate, Harv. Bus. Rev. July-August (1990) 104–112.

[23] M. Hammer, J. Champy, Reengineering the Corporation: A Manifestation for Business Revolution, Campus Fachbuch, seventh ed., 1996.

[24] R.S. Kaplan, D.P. Norton, The Balanced Scorecard: Translating Strategy into Action, Harvard Business School Press, 1996.

[25] D.J. Madison, Becoming A Process-Focused Organization, BPM Institute, http://www.bpminstitute.org/articles/article/article/becoming-a-process-focused-organization.html, 2007.

[26] M.A. Ould, Business Process Management: A Rigorous Approach, Meghan-Kiffer Press, 2005.

[27] G.A. Rummler, A.P. Brache, Improving Performance: How to Manage the White Space in the Organization Chart, Jossey-Bass, second ed., 1995.

[28] J. Siegel, In OMG's OCEB Certification Program, What Is the Definition of Business Process? http://www.omg.org/oceb/defbusinessprocess.htm, 2008.

[29] B. Silver, Three Levels of Process Modeling with BPMN, BPMS Watch, http://www.brsilver.com/wordpress/subscribers-only-2/three-levels-of-process-modeling-with-bpmn, April 2008.

[30] A. Smith, The Wealth of Nations, Anaconda, 2009.

[31] H. Smith, P. Fingar, Business Process Management: The Third Wave, Meghan Kiffer, 2006.

[32] S. Stralser, MBA in a Day, Wiley, 2004.

[33] A UML profile for MARTE, http://www.omg.org/cgi-bin/doc?realtime/07-03-03, 2007.

[34] L. Verner, The Challenge of Process Discovery, BPTrends. http://www.businessprocesstrends.com/deliverfile.cfm?-fileType=publication&fileName=05-04WPProcessDiscovery-Verner1.pdf, May 2004.

[35] E. Walters, What Are CSFs and KPIs? http://www.12manage.com/methodsrockartcsfskpis.html, July 2011.

[36] T. Weilkiens, Systems Engineering with SysML/UML, dpunkt.verlag, second ed., 2008. http://www.elsevier.com/wps/find/bookdescription.cws_home/713901/description#description.

# Index

Note: Page numbers followed by *b* indicate boxes, *f* indicate figures and *t* indicate tables.

# RECEIVE 10% OFF YOUR OCEB FUNDAMENTAL CERTIFICATION!

*You've already got the book -- take the next step
and register for your OCEB Fundamental exam today!*

**Why You Should Get Your OCEB Certification:**

- Credentials are important in the BPM world, where practitioners may work on many projects for different clients or employers over time.
- The twenty-five experts from top BPM companies and well-known independent consultants who designed the OCEB topical coverage and wrote the exam questions want peers and prospective employers to feel confident about a certified candidate's ability to participate in or lead real-world initiatives in enterprise BPM.
- Your status as an OCEB Certified Professional shows that you have the required knowledge and skills, making you a more attractive candidate for hiring and promotion.

**How to Register for Your Discounted Exam:**

- Go to the OMG Exam Registration page at Pearson VUE: http://pearsonvue.com/omg. Exams are available worldwide!
- You can locate a test center on the OMG registration page at Pearson VUE by clicking on "Locate a Test Center."
- Once you are ready, click on "schedule a test" on the OMG Registration page at Pearson VUE.
- Use the unique discount code below at checkout to save 10% off your certification exam.

Purchase the *OCEB Certification Guide* and become certified through OMG® and proudly display your qualifications by including the OMG Certification logo on your business cards, on your resume, and online!
At your option, display your certification in the OMG Certified Professionals Directory!

---

# 10% Discount Coupon
RECEIVE 10% OFF YOUR OCEB
FUNDAMENTAL CERTIFICATION!
Special Book Buyer's Code:

sW7y3swA